The Christmas search

A pageant of carols, narrative and mime

compiled by June B. Tillman

Cambridge University Press

Cambridge

New York Port Chester Melbourne Sydney

Other **SONGBOOKS** and **MUSICAL ACTIVITY BOOKS** published by Cambridge University Press

Light the candles!

Songs of praise and ceremony from around the world compiled by June B. Tillman
ISBN 0 521 33969 3

Seasonal songs

A collection of easy-to-learn songs for each season of the year with ideas for spin-off work. By Dot Paxton.
ISBN 0 521 33668 6

Story, song and dance

For the young, a collection of ideas for improvised drama with music, compiled by Jean Gilbert

Book   ISBN 0 521 33967 7
Cassette   ISBN 0 521 32758 X

Music through topics

An activity resource book for teachers of 4–8 year olds, by Veronica Clark

Book   ISBN 0 521 34842 0
Cassette   ISBN 0 521 35630 X

Titles in the **Cambridge YOUNG MUSICALS** series

The Bells of Lyonesse

Complete Production edition ISBN 0 521 33590 6

Seaspell

Piano/Conductor edition ISBN 0 521 33588 4
Performers' edition ISBN 0 521 33589 2

Duffy and the devil

Piano/Conductor edition ISBN 0 521 33592 2
Performers' edition ISBN 0 521 33593 0

African Madonna

Complete Production edition ISBN 0 521 37880 X

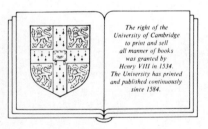

The right of the University of Cambridge to print and sell all manner of books was granted by Henry VIII in 1534. The University has printed and published continuously since 1584.

Published by the Press Syndicate of the University of Cambridge
The Pitt Building, Trumpington Street, Cambridge CB2 1RP
32 East 57th Street, New York, NY 10022, USA
10 Stamford Road, Oakleigh, Melbourne 3166, Australia

© Cambridge University Press 1989

First published 1989

Printed in Great Britain by Bell and Bain Ltd., Glasgow

Designed by Angela King
Illustrated by Gabrielle Stoddart

British Library cataloguing in publication data
The Christmas search: a pageant of carols,
   narrative and mime.
   1. Christmas carols in English. Words –
   Anthologies – For children
   I. Tillman, June
   783.6'52

ISBN 0 521 33968 5

The Christmas search
A pageant of carols, narrative and mime

The long journey made by the Three Magi in search of the Christ-child gave June Tillman the idea for a pageant of carols, narrative and mime organised around the theme of searching at Christmas.

The seventy carols come from all round the world – some old favourites of course, but many fresh new songs too, and from unusual sources. They are collected under topic headings that include both sacred and secular aspects of Christmas, and are arranged for piano and/or guitar. Many have simple pitched and unpitched percussion parts. There are also some parts for descant recorders (most of these use only the notes G, A and B, but a few use C and D as well). The accompaniments are very straightforward and most songs can even be sung unaccompanied.

As much information as possible on the origins of the carols is given. The staging could consist of a gradual building up of the Nativity scene, to which aspects of Christmas customs are added; but teachers can decide on the best staging for the resources they have and the scale of the presentation.

The narratives are intended to introduce the carols, and they can be rewritten in children's own words. Some of the stories briefly outlined in them could be expanded into complete plays; themes such as the search of King Arthur or space exploration could be extended into longer projects.

With its rich variety of carols, the accompanying narrative and suggestions for mime, dance and classwork, *The Christmas search* can be used either in the course of the normal school day or, by selecting and developing items to suit, for producing a pageant at Christmas.

Author's acknowledgements

Many people have helped with this collection. I am grateful to all the contributors of songs, especially David Moses, Cynthia Raza and Monica Shelton, who have contributed several, some specially for this collection. I am grateful to Ella Samuel for singing the Urdu Carol to me, to Juanita Ali for information on Christmas in Trinidad, and Jenny Fowler for help with the Australian carols. I am grateful to the Head Teacher, Ann Wilkins, and to the pupils and staff of Furzedown Primary School in South London, where the original project was tried out. I am grateful to my son Richard for allowing me to use a song written originally for his birthday. Finally, I should like to thank my husband and children for their patience.

JUNE TILLMAN

Publisher's acknowledgements

Many of the songs in this book are in copyright. For details, please refer first to the page on which the song appears. If application is made in writing, the Permissions Controller of Cambridge University Press will endeavour to forward correspondence regarding permissions to private individuals. The following is a list of songs which is in the copyright of publishers and other institutions. They may be contacted direct.

Every effort has been made to reach copyright holders, the publishers would be glad to hear from anyone whose rights they have unknowingly infringed.

2 *Five little snowmen*
Words and music by David B. Walden and Lois Birkenshaw. Used by permission of Berandol Music.

5 *The day that Christ was born on*
Words by John Wheeler, Music by William G. James. © 1948 Chappell Music Ltd, London W1Y 3FA. Reproduced by permission of Chappell Music Ltd and International Music Publications.

6 *Bring the sleigh*
Words by John Emlyn Edwards, c/o David Higham Associates Ltd, London. From *Follow my Leader* by Douglas Gillies, published by Oxford University Press.

9 *Advent candles*
Words by Emily Chisholm. Used by permission of Stainer and Bell Ltd, London.

10 *Baboushka*
Words by Arthur Scholey, Music by Donald Swann, © Scholey and Swann 1977. Used by permission of Roberton Publications, Aylesbury, England, for Albert House Press.

13 *Jog along, little donkey*
Words and music by Sister Mary Oswin. © 1968 Sister Mary Oswin. Reprinted from *Let God's Children Sing* by permission of Geoffrey Chapman, a division of Cassell Publishers Ltd, Artillery House, Artillery Row, London SW1 1RT.

19 *Jesus is crying*
Traditional Brazilian words adapted by Ann Mendoza. From *Sociable Carols* by Ann Mendoza and Patrick Shaw, © Oxford University Press 1979. Reproduced by kind permission of Oxford University Press.

20 *While Mary washed linen*
An Italian folk rhyme translated by Elizabeth Poston. From *The Children's Songbook* (song listed under the title 'The Holy Family'), published by The Bodley Head, London.

22 *Jesus, baby Jesus*
Words and music by Alice M. Pullen. From *The Nursery Song and Picture Book*, edited by Winifred E. Barnard, Religious and Moral Education Press, Exeter, England.

24 *There was a pig*
A traditional Lancashire children's carol, arranged by Allen Percival. From *The Galliard Book of Carols*. Reproduced by kind permission of Stainer and Bell Ltd, London.

33 *Follow the star*
From *Folksongs of Africa*. With thanks to Wolverhampton Education Committee.

36 *A holy baby*
Words by Tom Colvin, © Wild Goose Publications, The Iona Community, Bath, England.

38 *Carol of the drum*
Traditional Czech. Arranged by Douglas Coombes. From *More Songs for Singing Together* (song listed under the title 'The Little Drummer Boy'), published by BBC Books.

39 *The orchestra carol*
Words by Ann Mendoza and Pat Shaw. From *Sociable Carols* by Ann Mendoza and Patrick Shaw, © Oxford University Press 1979. Reproduced by kind permission of Oxford University Press.

40 *Carol of the birds*
Words by John Wheeler, Music by William G. James. © 1948 Chappell Music Ltd, London W1Y 3FA. Reproduced by permission of Chappell Music Ltd and International Music Publications.

41 *Bom, bom, bom!*
Traditional Chilean, collected by Jean Chapman for *The Sugar-Plum Song Book*, published by Hodder & Stoughton (Australia) Pty Ltd, 1977.

45 *In the stable*
Words by Hilda Rostron, Music by Colin Peters, from *New Child Songs*. Reproduced by permission of the National Christian Education Council, Redhill, Surrey, England.

47 *I have got a Christmas gift*
Words and music by Monica Shelton. From *Round the Seasons* by Monica Shelton, published by Basil Blackwell, Oxford.

51 *Gatatumba*
Words by Ann Mendoza. From *Sociable Carols* by Ann Mendoza and Patrick Shaw, © Oxford University Press 1979. Reproduced by kind permission of Oxford University Press.

54 *I am a pine tree*
Words and music by Louise B. Scott, © 1954 Bowmar. A Division of Belwin Mills. Used by permission.

55 *In forests dark*
Words by B. Charlesworth, Music by H. Bates. Used by permission of Scunthorpe Teachers' Centre RE Music Group, Scunthorpe, England.

56 *The whole world is a Christmas tree*
Words by Arthur Leon Moore. From *The World Sings*, published by A & C Black (publishers) Ltd, Eaton Socon, England.

57 *Carol for Christingle*
Words by Fred Pratt Green. From *The Galliard Book of Carols*. Reproduced by kind permission of Stainer and Bell Ltd, London.

62 *Christmas Bells*
Words and music by Zoe McHenry. From *The Sugar-Plum Song Book of Christmas Songs*, collected by Jean Chapman, published by Hodder & Stoughton (Australia) Pty Ltd, 1977.

63 *I am Father Christmas*
Words and music by Monica Shelton. From *Round the Seasons* by Monica Shelton, published by Basic Blackwell, London.

64 *When Santa got stuck up the chimney*
Words and music by Jimmy Grafton. Used by permission of Southern Music Publishing Company Ltd. 8 Denmark Street, London WC2.

66 *Christmas Eve in Trinidad*
Words and music by Massie Patterson and Sammy Heyward, © 1963 TRO Essex Music Limited, 19/20 Poland Street, London, W1V 3DD. International Copyright Secured. All Rights Reserved. Used by Permission. For Australia, reproduced by kind permission of Essex Music of Australia Pty Ltd.

67 *It's Christmas Day*
An adaptation by June Tillman of Huddie Ledbetter's 'It's almost day', © 1951 (Renewed 1979) and 1959 Folkways Music Publishers Inc. Assigned to TRO Essex Music Limited, 19/20 Poland Street, London, W1V 3DD. International Copyright Secured. All Rights Reserved. Used by Permission.

Contents

The search for hope   7
Making preparations   17
The search for a room   27
A helping hand   35
The search for the baby   49
The journey to worship   65
Giving presents   77
Plays, carols and cribs   91
Decorations and cards   101
Christmas customs   113
Parties and food   121

The Christmas search

Narrative

Have you ever searched hard for anything you needed or wanted? Christmas is a time for searching – Mary and Joseph search for a room, the Wise Men search for the baby, and everyone makes preparations for the festive season. This pageant looks at all these searches.

Searching jingle

This little jingle can be used throughout the pageant as a recurring motif to remind the audience of the theme.

Words and music by
June Tillman

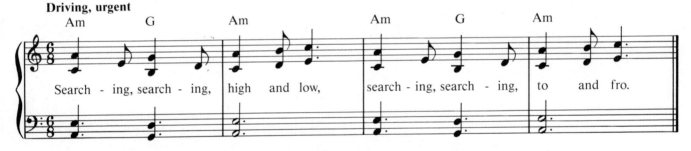

Driving, urgent

Search - ing, search - ing, high and low, search - ing, search - ing, to and fro.

Chime bars

The search for hope

1 This is the way
2 Five little snowmen
3 Troika
4 Tell me, what month was my Jesus born in?
5 The day that Christ was born on
6 Bring the sleigh

1
This is the way

Narrative

Long before the birth of Christ and the celebration of Christmas, people searched for hope in the dark, days of winter. They celebrated midwinter festivals. On the shortest day people worshipped the sun and prayed for it to come back. In Northern Europe cattle were killed and bonfires were lit. This was to tell people that the sun would appear again. A yule log was burned.

There were many customs in Northern Europe that went with the burning of the yule log. It was often lit on Christmas Eve with carefully washed hands and would burn throughout the 12 days of Christmas. In Cornwall children were allowed to sit up till midnight on Christmas Eve to drink to the log.

In Devon the oak log was bound with nine bands of ash wood. The unmarried girls would each choose a band. The person whose band burst first would be the first to marry. In some places a small piece of the log was kept through the year to protect the house from thunder and lightning and some of the ashes would be mixed with the corn to be sown in the spring.

In some countries felling the log was a time of great excitement. In Yugoslavia oak trees were cut and women decorated them with red ribbons and gold wire. As the log was dragged home candles were lit on the way. In some places in Europe the number of sparks that flew up when the log burned was thought to show how many children and animals would arrive in the household that year.

In Lerwick in the Shetland Islands there is a dramatic sight on the last Tuesday in January. A huge Viking ship, painted red, blue and gold, is towed through the streets. Warriors' shields hang from it. Men dressed in Viking costumes carry flaming torches beside it. Then it is set on fire. The custom comes from the Viking fire festival and now it is a time when people have parties and enjoy themselves.

Traditional, adapted by
Lucille Wood and June Tillman

Brightly

1. This is the way the snow comes down, Snow comes down, snow comes down. This is the way the snow comes down, On a win-ter day.

2 This is the way it covers the town, etc.

3 This is the way the cold winds blow, etc.

4 This is the way we cut the log, etc.

5 This is the way we drag home the log, etc.

6 This is the way we light the log, etc.

7 This is the way the flames leap up, etc.

Suggestion

This could also be a song just about the snow. Use the first two verses and then add some of your own about shovelling, rolling and throwing snow.

Accompaniment

Drum

Snow   comes down

Add an Indian cymbal on the beat.

2
Five little snowmen

Narrative

Building a snowman is a fun thing to do after there's been a heavy snowfall even though your hands get really freezing cold. Stones and bits of wood make good eyes, noses, mouths and buttons. If you lend him your scarf or hat he really will look like a person. And then, when the sun shines and your snowman begins to melt away. . . well, you'll feel just a little bit sad.

Words and music by
David B. Walden and Lois
Birkenshaw

1. Five lit - tle snow - men in a row, Five lit - tle snow - men made of snow,

Out came the sun and shone all day, One lit - tle snow - man mel - ted a - way.

2 Four little snowmen, etc.

3 Three little snowmen, etc.

4 Two little snowmen, etc.

5 One little snowmen, etc.

6 No little snowmen, etc.

Activity

Five children stand in a row as the snowmen. Another child acts the sun and shines on them. S/he puts her/his arms round each snowman and s/he melts into a puddle on the floor.

Accompaniment

Add a drum playing

Five lit - tle snow - men

Repeat throughout.

3
Troika

Narrative

The jingling of the bells of the sleigh may be to drive
away the spirits of darkness. Imagine the scene as
the sleigh glides through the night with the snow
and ice sparkling and the horses' bells jingling.

Music traditional Russian,
arranged by June Tillman

The dance

A troika is a Russian sleigh drawn by three horses, and it is sets of three 'horses' who perform this exuberant dance.

The three horses line up side by side, close to each other, holding hands and lifting them up in the air, as if they are hitched to the sleigh with a high harness. All the horses, in sets of three, form a long line.

Measures 1–4: The horses run forward eight steps, lifting their knees up high in a kind of prance. Then they take eight prancing steps back to where they started, still lifting their knees high in front, even though they are going backwards.

Measures 5 and 6: The two horses on the left (A and B), still holding hands, raise their arms in the air to form an arch. The horse on the right (C) runs eight steps under the arch and back to place, pulling B under the arch too. A takes running steps in place. (In a more complicated version, A can turn under his or her own arm).

Measures 7 and 8: Repeat the same step as in the previous two measures, but this time B and C form the arch and A runs under it, pulling B along. C runs in place. Then all three horses form a circle.

Measures 9–11: The horses take 12 running steps to the left, pulling away from each other.

Measures 12: They stamp three times, hard, in place and pause.

Measures 13–15: They reverse and run 12 counts in the opposite direction.

Measures 16: They stamp three times, straighten out the line on the last count, and are ready to start the dance again.

Since there is so much running, this is a tiring dance (good for rainy days), but most 'horses' want to repeat it several times.

Accompaniment

Chime bars

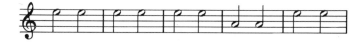

A descant recorder could play the tune. Claves or coconut shells could play on the beat and bells could play

4
Tell me, what month was my Jesus born in?

Narrative

Was the 25th of December really the birthday of Jesus? No one knows. The Church leaders searched hard before they decided on this day for the date of Christmas. The 25th of December was finally fixed upon by Pope Julius I, who lived about 1600 years ago. Before that it had been the first and the sixth of January, the 29th of March and the 29th of September. December was chosen probably to help people to think of Jesus as the Light of the World in the dark days of winter.

Capo 3rd fret
With bounce
VERSE

Traditional American

1. Tell me, what month was my Je - sus born in? Last month of the year.— Tell me what month was my Je - sus born in? Last— month of the

CHORUS

year. Well you got Jan - u - a - ry, Feb - ru - a - ry, March, Oh— Lord,— you got—

A - pril, May and June, Lord, you got Ju - ly, Au-gust, Sep - tem - ber, Oc - to - ber and— No-

vem - ber, You got the twen-ty-fifth day of De - cem - ber, Last— month of the year.

2   He was born in an ox-stall manger,
     Last month of the year.   } *Twice*

     CHORUS   Well you got January, etc.

3   Yes, I'm talking about Mary's baby,
     Last month of the year.   } *Twice*

     CHORUS   Well you got January, etc.

Suggestion

This carol can be extended to tell the whole story
with verses like 'Shepherds on the hillside all saw
an angel' and 'Hang up the holly and the mistletoe
bough'.

Accompaniment

Add lively percussion parts to this:

month   was   my   Je - sus   born   in

Repeat throughout.

5
The day that Christ was born on

Narrative

Not all parts of the world celebrate Christmas in the winter. In the tropical countries of Africa, Asia, the Pacific and the Caribbean there are no seasons of summer and winter. It is hot all the year round, with usually a dry season and a rainy season. In the southern hemisphere Christmas falls in the summer. Here is a carol from Australia. It talks about summer in the outback – the open grasslands where there are many large farms. In verse 4 the moon is said to have a 'chalice' – a special kind of cup.

Capo 3rd fret

Brightly

Words by John Wheeler
Music by William G. James

1. When the sun's a gol - den rose, And the mag - pie ca - rols clear, You can say, and I can say, On the sum - mer mor - ning, Here at last is Christ-mas Day, The day that Christ was born on, The day that

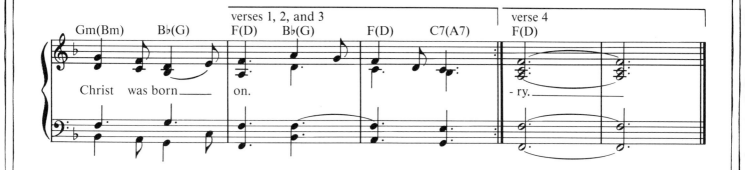

2   When the wand'ring, lonely sheep,
Find at last a shady pool,
You can say, and I can say,
On the outback station,
Here at last is Christmas Day,
The day Christ brought salvation,
The day Christ brought salvation.

3   When the ranges turn to flame,
And the winds like trumpets blow,
You can say, and I can say,
Seven times and seven,
Here at last is Christmas Day,
The day Christ came from heaven,
The day Christ came from heaven.

4   But when summer's shining moon,
Dips a silver chalice bright,
You can say, and I can say,
Joyously and airy,
Here at last is Christmas Day,
The day Christ smiled at Mary,
The day Christ smiled at Mary.

Accompaniment

The guitar chords do not fit with the piano part.
Add a different instrument for each line. Let them all
play together on line 7. Suggestions are a cymbal for
line 1, a triangle for line 2, a drum for line 3, an
Indian cymbal for line 4, a tambourine for line 5,
castanets for line 6. The children may have other
suggestions.

6
Bring the sleigh

Narrative

Travelling by horse-drawn sleigh is one way of riding around in thick snow. The riders glide peacefully over the snow snugly wrapped in furs.

Words by John Emlyn Edwards
Music traditional Russian,
arranged by June Tillman

2 Wrapped in furs, all snug and warm,
   Now everybody's cosy,
   Not a care
   For the wintry air
   That makes our faces rosy.

3 Swiftly, through the silent forest,
   Ponies trotting lightly,
   Watch us streak
   To the mountain peak,
   With sleigh bells jingling brightly.

4 High we'll fly to reach the sky where
   Winter's moon is hiding,
   Up we'll go
   Over clouds of snow,
   Our sleigh for ever riding.

Suggestion

Talk about the difficulty of moving about in snowy countries. Discuss methods like ski-ing and skating. Look at paintings of sleighs of different kinds, such as those used in Antarctic expeditions (comparing Scott's and Amundsen's use of sleighs, for example) and those that appear in such fairy tales as 'The Snow Queen'. Then compare these with modern snow-scooters and snowmobiles.

Accompaniment

Pitched percussion

Add sleigh bells and claves or wood block playing quavers.

Making preparations

7   Dame get up and bake your pies
8   Play, musicians
9   Advent candles
10   Baboushka
11   Christmas calypso

7
Dame get up and bake your pies

Narrative

Many of the midwinter festivals involved feasting, decorating houses, giving presents and having parties. All these things needed preparation. In the weeks leading up to Christmas everyone gets very busy. This traditional carol lists some of the things the 'dame' had to do to get ready.

Cakes, sweetmeats, gingerbread and marzipan were traditional foods. Mince pies were originally meat pies. They were oval to represent the manger Jesus was born in. Gradually they became the sweet pies containing sugar, peel, almonds, suet and apples that we know today.

Our Christmas pudding became popular in the nineteenth century. Before that time, people ate plum porridge, which was made by boiling beef and mutton with broth thickened with bread-crumbs, raisins, currants and prunes and sea-soned with spices, cloves and ginger. It was eaten with a spoon as a meat course.

Capo 3rd fret

With vigour

Traditional, arranged by
June Tillman

2 Dame, what makes your maidens lie? etc.

3 Dame, what makes your ducks to die? etc.

4 Their wings are cut and they cannot fly, etc.

5 Dame, get up and sweep the floor, etc.

6 Dame, get up, invite your friend, etc.

Suggestion

Add other verses with things that the dame might do. Dance it as a circle dance doing the appropriate actions.

Accompaniment

Add a drum playing

Bake your pies

Repeat throughout.

Chime bars

8
Play, musicians

Narrative

In various parts of the world travelling musicians traditionally tour the town the week before Christmas searching for a welcome. In England they are called waits.

Waits used to play popular tunes on wind instruments. In Pickering in Yorkshire the 'shouter' calls at each house 'Good morning, Mr Brown! Good morning, Mrs Brown! Happy Christmas to your household! Past two o'clock and a fine morning.'

Mr and Mrs Brown come to their door and carols are sung. Sometimes the waits are offered a drink.

Before the days of alarm clocks, watchmen used to go round the town every morning waking people up, and the waits' custom goes back to this time.

In Italy, shepherds and children dressed as shepherds also go round playing. They too are invited in for money and drinks. They are called pipers or *pifferai*.

Words and music by
Pamela Verrall

Blow the trum-pet, Beat that drum, Cas-ta-nets and sound-ing cym-bals,

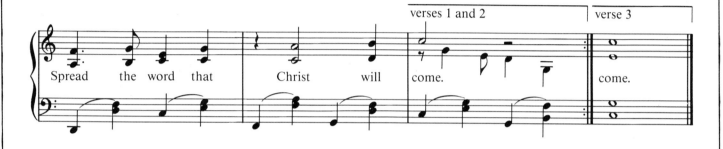

verses 1 and 2   verse 3

Spread the word that Christ will come.   come.

2   Have you heard what people say?
He's expected any day,
Guided by a brilliant light,
Star of Bethl'em, burning bright.

     CHORUS   So play, musicians, etc.

3   Go and see the Holy Boy,
Go with all your love and joy.
Gaze with wonder on His face
When you find that Holy Place.

     CHORUS   So play, musicians, etc.

Activity

Make a collage of the baby Jesus surrounded by the instruments of the orchestra.

Accompaniment

Add the instruments mentioned in the song.

Drum

Blow the trum-pet

Castanets

Cymbal

21

9
Advent candles

Narrative

Christians who go to church regularly prepare for the coming of Jesus during the four weeks of Advent. In some churches an advent wreath is made. This is a circle of evergreens in which are placed four red candles. On each Sunday in Advent one more candle is lighted and a different person in the story remembered in a song. In the middle is a large white candle which is lighted on Christmas Day to show that Christ has come.

In Finland the four advent candles are placed beneath a decoration of metal angels. As the candles burn the angels turn.

Words by Emily Chisholm
Music traditional Welsh,
arranged by June Tillman

1. The hol-ly and the i - vy, Are danc-ing in a ring, Round the

ber-ry bright red can - dles, And the white and shi - ning King.

2 And one is for God's people,
  In every age and day.
  We are watching for his coming.
  We believe and we obey.

3 Oh, two is for the prophets,
  And for the light they bring.
  They are candles in the darkness,
  All alight for Christ the King.

4 And three for John the Baptist,
  He calls on us to sing:

  'O prepare the way for Jesus Christ,
  He is coming, Christ the King.'

5   And four for Mother Mary,
    'I cannot see the way,
    But you promise me a baby.
    I believe you. I obey.'

6   And Christ is in the centre,
    For this is his birthday.
    With the shining nights of Christmas
    Singing, 'He has come today.'

Suggestion

This song is designed to accompany the custom of the advent wreath. On each of the four Sundays before Christmas one verse is sung. Then, on Christmas Day, all the verses are sung. During the singing the candles are gradually lighted. Here is a set of readings that can be used to precede the song. One set of readings goes with each Sunday:

The Advent candles

1 Introduction:
  The first candle represents all God's faithful people. It is for the light of Jesus which we bring to the world today. St Peter says of us:

  You are a chosen race, a royal priesthood, God's own people chosen to proclaim the wonderful acts of him who called you out of darkness into his marvellous light.

2 Introduction:
  The second candle is for the prophets and for the light they give. The prophet Isaiah looks forward to the light that Jesus will bring to the world:

  I will make you a light to the nations, to be my salvation to earth's farthest bounds.

3 Introduction:
  The third candle represents John the Baptist. He too looks forward to the light that Jesus brings to the world. The apostle John, a close friend of Jesus, writes this of John the Baptist:

  God sent his messenger, a man named John, who came to tell people about the light.

4 Introduction:
  The fourth candle represents Mary. Because she was ready to obey God's will and be the mother of Jesus, the Light of the World, she says:

  My heart praises the Lord. From now on people will call me happy because of the great things the mighty God has done for me.

5 Introduction:
  Today we light the fifth candle, the large white one. This is for Jesus, who was born into the world on Christmas Day to give us all light.

  Jesus said, I am the Light of the World. No follower of mine shall wander in the dark; he shall have the light of life.

Accompaniment

Add an Indian cymbal on the first beat of each bar.

Pitched percussion

Descant recorders

10
Baboushka

Narrative

In the middle of all this getting ready we must not forget about a legend from Russia. It is all about being too busy to go and see Jesus.

Baboushka was so busy cleaning and tidying that she told the three Wise Men to go on without her. She said that she would follow when she had finished her work. By the time she reached Bethlehem the baby Jesus had been taken by Mary and Joseph to safety in Egypt.

Some versions of the story have her still searching for the baby Jesus; in this carol she finds Jesus in her heart. Another version of the story has her looking for good children to be rewarded with sweets and gifts at Epiphany. When she finds disobedient ones she leaves a switch (a tree branch) and a lump of coal in their stockings.

Words by Arthur Scholey
Music by Donald Swann

far?' 'Ba - boush - ka, oh, Ba - boush - ka, we're fol - low - ing a

star. Ba - boush - ka, oh, Ba - boush - ka, we're fol - low - ing a star.'

2

'The star's a mighty marvel,
A truly glorious sight.
But, Lords, you must stay longer –
Oh, won't you stay the night?
Do tell me why you hurry –
And here's another thing:
I marvel at the meaning of the precious gifts you bring.'

'Baboushka, oh, Baboushka, they're for a new-born king.
Baboushka, oh, Baboushka, they're for a new-born king.'

3

'Some king, to have such treasures,
A star to show his birth,
And you to do him honour,
The greatest ones of earth.
'And yet he is a baby,
A tiny man is he?
O Royal Ones, I wonder, then, if he will welcome me?'

'Baboushka, oh, Baboushka, oh, why not come and see?
Baboushka, oh, Baboushka, oh, why not come and see?'

4

'I will, my Royal Masters –
But not just now, I fear.
I'll follow on tomorrow
When I have finished here.
My home I must make tidy,
And sweep and polish, too,
And then some gifts I must prepare – I have so much to do!'

'Baboushka, oh, Baboushka, we dare not wait for you.
Baboushka, oh, Baboushka, we dare not wait for you.'

Suggestion

This song provides an excellent framework for acting the story.

5

At last I make the journey
No star to lead me on.
'Good people, can you tell me
The way the Kings have gone?'
Some shepherds tell of angels
But now there is no sound.
The stable, it is empty, and the baby Egypt-bound.

'Baboushka, oh, Baboushka, we know where he is found.
Baboushka, oh, Baboushka, we know where he is found.'

6

Through all the years I seek him
I feel him very near.
O people, do you know him?
Oh, tell me: Is he here?
In all the world I travel
But late I made my start.
Oh, tell me if you find him for I've searched in every part.

'Baboushka, oh, Baboushka, we find him in our heart.
Baboushka, oh, Baboushka, we find him in our heart.'

Accompaniment

Use a drum to accompany verse 1 in the rhythm

‖ ♩ ♫ ‖ , an Indian cymbal in verse 2 in

‖ ♩ ♩ ‖ , a drum in verse 3 in ‖ ♩ ♫ ‖ ,

a wood block in verse 4 in ‖ ♫ ♫ ‖ , a tam-

bourine in verse 5 in the rhythm ‖ ♫ ♫ ‖

and a triangle in verse 6 in ‖ ♩ ♩ ‖

25

11
Christmas calypso

Narrative

Today we still get busy before Christmas, just as people in the past used to do. Searching for the right present for everyone is just one of the things to do, and many others are listed in this song. Christmas puddings and cakes are traditionally prepared on the Sunday nearest St Andrew's Day (1st December). This is called 'Stir up' Sunday because its special prayer started: 'Stir up, O Lord, the wills of your faithful people'. People wish as they stir the pudding. Sometimes lucky charms or money are put in.

Words by Wendy Bird
Music adapted by Wendy Bird

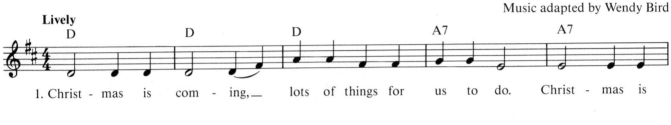

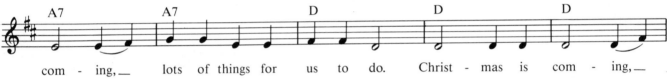

2 Christmas is coming, mix your Christmas puddings.

Christmas is coming, mix your Christmas puddings.

Christmas is coming, stir it round and make a wish.

Christmas is coming, mix your Christmas puddings.

3 Christmas is coming, bake your cake and make your pies.
Christmas is coming, bake your cake and make your pies.
Christmas is coming, put them in the oven.
Christmas is coming, bake your cake and make your pies.

4 Christmas is coming, decorate your houses.

Christmas is coming, decorate your houses.
Christmas is coming, paper chains and holly.

Christmas is coming, decorate your houses.

Suggestion

This can be extended to cover many Christmas preparations. Create a play around the idea of a busy mother at her wits' end, trying to get everything ready.

The search for a room

12 How many miles to Bethlehem?
13 Jog along, little donkey
14 No room at the inn
15 Kokoleoko
16 Christmas night a star shine-o

12
How many miles to Bethlehem?

Narrative

There are lots of people searching in the Christmas story. First of all, Mary and Joseph had to make the long journey from Nazareth to Bethlehem. It would have taken them four or five days.

Words by Irene Babsky
Music by Irene Babsky,
arranged by Diana Thompson

1. Jo - seph, __ oh Jo - seph I'm wea - ry to __ my bones __

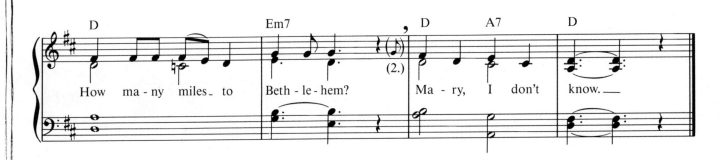

How ma - ny miles __ to Beth - le - hem? (2.) Ma - ry, I don't know. __

2 Mary, oh Mary, I'll help you all I can.

When our baby boy is born

He'll grow to be a man.

3 Joseph, oh Joseph, is there far to go?
   How many miles to Bethlehem?
   Mary, I don't know.

4 Mary, oh Mary, I will love him so.
   How many miles to Bethlehem?
   Mary, I don't know.

Suggestion

This carol can be sung as two solos or with one group of children for Mary and one for Joseph.

Accompaniment

Choose one instrument to accompany Mary and one for Joseph.

Pitched percussion

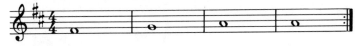

Descant recorders

13
Jog along, little donkey

Narrative

There were no trains and buses in those days, so the family had to use a donkey to carry Mary and their belongings. Try to imagine what it would have been like for the donkey. Did he get tired too? Did he know the baby was to be special or was he angry about being chosen for such a long journey?

Words and music by
Sister Mary Oswin

1. Jog a - long, lit - tle don - key to Beth - le - hem, Though it's a ve - ry long ride.
(3.)

Jog a - long ta - king Ma - ry to Beth - le - hem; Jo - seph will walk there by your side.

2. At the end there's a sta - ble for shel - ter And plen - ty of hay so you'll be fed.

Save a bit for the babe who'll be born to - night, For he will have no o - ther bed.

3 Jog along, little donkey to Bethlehem;
We are so grateful to you.
God's light streams from the stable in Bethlehem;
In there his promise has come true.

Accompaniment

Accompany this with claves and bells.

14
No room at the inn

Narrative

The roads at that time were not like ours. They would have been bare earth. They would not have been smooth but would have had deep ruts made by animals' feet. The rain would have made deep channels down them. Robbers lurked in the hills and set upon passing travellers, as we hear in the story Jesus told called 'The Good Samaritan'. Mary and Joseph would have been frightened of such a long journey and even when they arrived in Bethlehem there was nowhere to stay. They searched desperately for a room.

Words and music by
Hazel Morfey

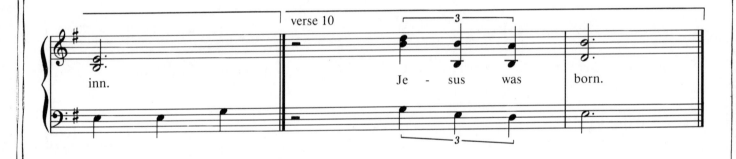

2   With heavy steps, she stumbled on,
    No room at the inn.

3   'Have courage, Mary', Joseph said,
    No room at the inn.

4   'For we will surely find a bed',
    No room at the inn.

5   'I am so tired I must lie down',
    No room at the inn.

6　'There must be somewhere in this town',
　　No room at the inn.

7　'Then we will shelter in this stable',
　　No room at the inn.

8　'Straw for your bed, stone for a table',
　　No room at the inn.

9　A baby's cry came through the night.
　　No longer forlorn.

10　The small dark cow-shed filled with light.
　　Jesus was born.

Activity

Make up a drama with lots of people all going
about their business, and Mary and Joseph trying
to find a way through them all.

Accompaniment

Chime bars

(Stop on the last two bars)

15
Kokoleoko

Narrative

We still remember Joseph and Mary's search today. In Mexico on the 16th of December and the days leading up to Christmas, families act out a ceremony called *Los Posadas*. A procession sets out. Two children lead the way. The others carry a platform (the *posada*) decorated with pine branches. On the platform stand statues of Mary and Joseph. Mary is sitting on a donkey. The procession goes all round the neighbourhood knocking at doors and asking to be let in.

After singing and praying at the *posada* in the chosen house comes fun with the *pinatas* – earthenware jars covered with coloured paper, containing nuts, sweets and fruit. They are hung in the streets and children go round looking for them. When a *pinata* is found the children put on a blindfold and are given a long stick, which they must use to break open the jar. The presents then shower down for everyone to have.

Mary and Joseph's search ended in a stable. We must not forget that in the world today there are lots of people who have no home. Especially at Christmas – which is a time for giving – we can remember these people and give something to those organisations that help them.

Traditional African song, adapted by David Evans

Gently

CHORUS

Ko-ko-le-o-ko, chick-en, ko-ko-le-o-ko, ko-ko-le-o-ko, chick-en, Crow-ing for day.

VERSE

1. Sun is ri-sing on Beth-le-hem, ko-ko-le-o-ko, chick-en, Crow-ing for day.

2 Mary and Joseph are searching for a room,
   Kokoleoko, chicken,
   Crowing for day.
   CHORUS   Kokoleoko, etc.

3 There is no room found in any of the inns, etc.
   CHORUS   Kokoleoko, etc.

4 Someone has found them a bare and rocky cave, etc.
   CHORUS   Kokoleoko, etc.

5 Baby Jesus born today, etc.
   CHORUS   Kokoleoko, etc.

6 Baby sleeps on a bed of hay, etc.
   CHORUS   Kokoleoko, etc.

7 Ox and ass there to keep him warm, etc.
   CHORUS   Kokoleoko, etc.

8 Shepherds come and they bring him a lamb, etc.
   CHORUS   Kokoleoko, etc.

9 Wise Men come with their precious gifts, etc.
   CHORUS   Kokoleoko, etc.

10 Everybody sing for joy, etc.
    CHORUS   Kokoleoko, etc.

11 Everybody clap for joy, etc.
    CHORUS   Kokoleoko, etc.

Alternative version

1 Santa Claus comes on Christmas night, etc.
   CHORUS   Kokoleoko, etc.

2 Hang your stockings at the end of your bed, etc.
   CHORUS   Kokoleoko, etc.

3 Have you told Santa what to bring? etc.
   CHORUS   Kokoleoko, etc.

4 I've got a drum and a big blue train, etc.
   CHORUS   Kokoleoko, etc.

Suggestion

Sing as many verses as are appropriate for your
pageant. The others can be used if you want to use
the song as the basis for an entire pageant.

Accompaniment

Pitched percussion

Repeat throughout

Repeat throughout

Unpitched percussion

ko - ko - le - o, ko - ko - le - o

Repeat throughout

Crow - ing for day

Repeat throughout

16
Christmas night a star shine-o

Narrative

High in the heavens a special star shone. Some people now think it might have been an appearance of Halley's Comet.

In Poland the appearance of the first star on Christmas Eve is an important event. It is time for the family meal. Before the meal, the head of the household breaks the Christmas wafer or *oplateki*. This has been blessed in church. Everybody is given a piece as a sign of peace and goodwill. Then follows a meal with 12 courses – one for each of Jesus' close friends. There is always a spare place at the table, so that any stranger may be immediately welcomed. When this is finally over, the children lie on a bed of straw to remind them of Christ's birth.

Words and music by
Cynthia Raza

1. Christ - mas night a star shine - o, Christ - mas night a ___ star shine - o,

Christ - mas night a star shine - o. Hi dum o did - dle lum pi o

2 Mary and Joseph to Bethlehem go, etc.

3 Baby born in a stable-o, etc.

4 Shepherds see the baby-o, etc.

5 Wise Men bring their presents-o, etc.

6 Peace on earth sing the angels-o, etc.

Suggestion

The whole story could be told from the point of view of the star. With extra verses added, the carol could form the basis of this.

Accompaniment

Use Indian cymbals to accompany the verse and shakers and tambourines for 'Hi dum o', etc.

Pitched percussion

Repeat throughout

Descant recorders

A helping hand

17   The friendly animals
18   Rocking carol
19   Jesus is crying
20   While Mary washed linen
21   Ibne Allah (lullaby)
22   Jesus, baby Jesus
23   Wind through the olive trees
24   There was a pig
25   The angel band

17
The friendly animals

Narrative

So Jesus was born in a stable. It was probably cold, dark and uncomfortable, but there were the animals to keep the family warm. This carol tells how the animals all helped Mary and Joseph in their search for a comfortable place to have the baby Jesus.

There is a legend about a spider who felt he had nothing to give to the baby. But when Mary and Joseph went to Egypt they sheltered in a cave. The spider spun a web across the entrance. When the soldiers came searching for the baby to kill him they saw that the web was not broken and decided that nobody was in the cave. And so the spider, in his own way, saved the baby Jesus.

Words traditional
Music traditional,
arranged by June Tillman

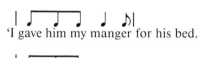

2 'I', said the donkey, all shaggy and brown,

'I carried his mother uphill and down.

I carried her safely to Bethlehem Town.

I', said the donkey, all shaggy and brown.

3 'I', said the sheep with the curly horn,

'I gave him my wool for a blanket warm.

He wore my coat on Christmas morn.

I', said the sheep with the curly horn.

4 'I', said the cow all white and red,

'I gave him my manger for his bed.

I gave him my hay to rest his head.

I', said the cow all white and red.

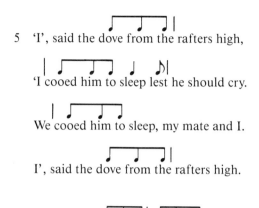

5 'I', said the dove from the rafters high,

'I cooed him to sleep lest he should cry.

We cooed him to sleep, my mate and I.

I', said the dove from the rafters high.

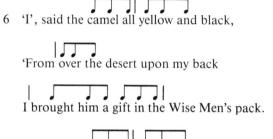

6 'I', said the camel all yellow and black,

'From over the desert upon my back

I brought him a gift in the Wise Men's pack.

I', said the camel all yellow and black.

7 Thus every beast by some good spell

In the stable dark was glad to tell

Of the gift he gave Emmanuel,

Of the gift he gave Emmanuel.

Activity
Make up a dance for each animal to do round the crib.

Accompaniment

Pitched percussion

Repeat throughout. Choose an instrument suitable for each animal to accompany each verse. The guitar chords do not fit with the keyboard part.

18
Rocking carol

Narrative

Mary and Joseph were a long way from their own home and their friends. Did they find friends in Bethlehem to help them with food and clothing for the baby? In this carol Joseph searches for clothing from local people.

In many parts of the world today people need food and clothing. You can help some of them by giving something – it doesn't matter if you can't afford very much – to charity.

Words traditional from
The Oxford Book of Carols
Music traditional Czech

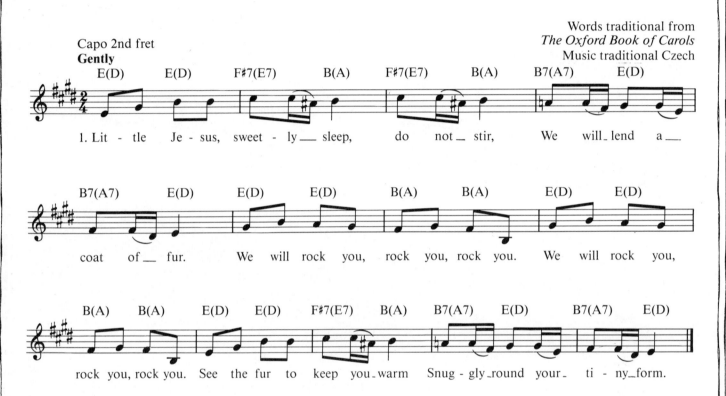

2   Mary's little baby sleep, sweetly sleep,
    Sleep in comfort, slumber deep,
    We will rock you, rock you, rock you,
    We will rock you, rock you, rock you,
    We will serve you all we can,
    Darling, darling little man.

Activity

Make up a rocking dance with big swaying movements – rocking the cradle, rocking the baby.

19
Jesus is crying

Narrative

Here it looks as if local people were offering Mary advice about how to soothe the baby Jesus. Mothers often search for advice when their baby is crying. What would you advise Mary to do?

Words adapted by Ann Mendoza
Music traditional Brazilian,
arranged by June Tillman

Lightly

A   E7   E7   A

1. Give Je - sus the ba - by some wa - ter, Ma - ri - a, O

A   E7   E7   A   A7   D

give him some wa - ter to cool him, Ma - ri - a, O give him some wa - ter for

E7   A   A7   D   E7   A

Je - sus is cry - ing, O give him some wa - ter so Je - sus will smile.

2   Give Jesus the baby a sweet drink, Maria,
O give him the juice of an orange, Maria,
O give him a sweet drink for Jesus is crying,
O give him a sweet drink so Jesus will smile.

3   Give Jesus the baby a rattle, Maria,
O give him a rattle to play with, Maria, etc.

4   Give Jesus the baby a bean bag, Maria,
O give him a bean bag to play with, Maria, etc.

Accompaniment

Choose a suitable unpitched instrument for each verse to suit the present.

Suggestion

Discuss the children's own experience of the arrival of a new baby and add more verses about the presents they might bring to make him/her happy.

Chime bars

20
While Mary washed linen

Narrative

In this Italian carol Mary, Joseph and Jesus are shown as a very ordinary family needing to wash and dry clothes. You can see them depicted like this in Italian paintings of the Holy Family. In Italy, people used to spread their washing to dry on the ground, walls and bushes. The writers of the carol see the family as being like themselves. If we look hard enough we can find ways in which Jesus' family is like our own and Jesus is like us.

Words collected and translated by
Elizabeth Poston. Music traditional Italian,
arranged by June Tillman

While Ma-ry washed li-nen, Jo-seph spread it dry-ing, The ba-by was sleep-y, And sore-ly was cry-ing, 'O hush you, my ba-by, For now I will tend you, I'll take you and I'll rock you And sing lul-la-by, I'll take you and I'll rock you And sing lul-la-by.'

Maria lavava,
Giuseppe tendeva,
Il bambino piangeva
Dal sonno che aveva.
Stai zitto, mio figlio,
Ch'adesso ti piglio,
Ti piglio e ti fascio
La nanna ti fo,
Ti piglio e ti fascio
La nanna ti fo.

Activity

Try painting a picture of baby Jesus with his mother
as if he had been born today.

Accompaniment

Pitched percussion

Repeat throughout.

21
Ibne Allah (lullaby)

Repeat the first line (* – *) at the end of the song.

Narrative

In this well-known Urdu carol Jesus is seen as a good baby, with the angels and stars all helping to comfort him.

Urdu carol collected
from Ella Samuel

Flowing

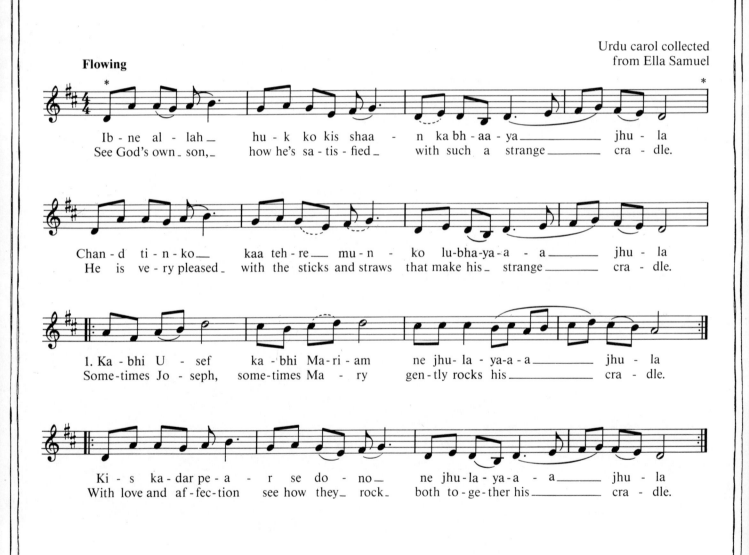

Ib - ne al - lah__ hu - k ko kis shaa - n ka bh-aa-ya_____ jhu - la
See God's own_ son,_ how he's sa - tis - fied_ with such a strange_____ cra - dle.

Chan - d ti - n-ko__ kaa teh - re__ mu - n - ko lu-bha-ya-a_____ jhu - la
He is ve - ry pleased_ with the sticks and straws that make his_ strange_____ cra - dle.

1. Ka - bhi U - sef ka - bhi Ma-ri - am ne jhu - la - ya-a_____ jhu - la
Some-times Jo - seph, some-times Ma - ry gen-tly rocks his_____ cra - dle.

Ki - s ka-dar pe - a - r se do - no_ ne jhu-la - ya - a_____ jhu - la
With love and af - fec - tion see how they_ rock_ both to - ge-ther his_____ cra - dle.

42

2 Loria mithi se kooch tehre su - la - ne   keliye (twice)

Kehekoosha or sureiya ne jhula-ya-a-a jhula. (twice)

3 Kiye Jabraieel ne firdos ke sub phool jama

Oon he phoolon se farishton ne sajaya-a-a jhula.

Ibne allah huk ko kis shaan ka bha-ya-a-a jhula.

---

2 He needs so few lullabies to make him gently sleep.

All the stars together – Milky Way and Mars – gently rock his cradle.

3 Now then Gabriel set out on his way for to find heavenly flowers;
And with all these flowers all the angels decorate his cradle.

See God's own son, how he's satisfied with such a strange cradle.

Activity

Make a collection of different pictures of the cradle
and add some of the children's own.

43

22
Jesus, baby Jesus

Narrative

Here is the traditional picture that we often see of Mary sitting and rocking Jesus in her arms. Do you think that is how it would have been? Many people have painted this scene. You will often see it on Christmas cards.

Words and music by
Alice Pullen

Je - sus, ba - by Je - sus, Mo-ther Ma - ry loves you, (3.) Rocks you to sleep.

2   Jesus, baby Jesus,
       Shepherds run to find you,
       Leaving their sheep.

3   Jesus, baby Jesus,
       Wise Men come to find you:
       ♪|
       A star leads the way.

4   Jesus, baby Jesus,
       All the children love you,
       Love Christmas Day.

Suggestion

With new verses added, this carol can be used to tell the whole Christmas story.

Accompaniment

Pitched percussion

Wind through the olive trees

Narrative

In this carol the wind blows softly round the stable
while the angels sing joyful songs.

Words traditional
Music traditional,
arranged by June Tillman

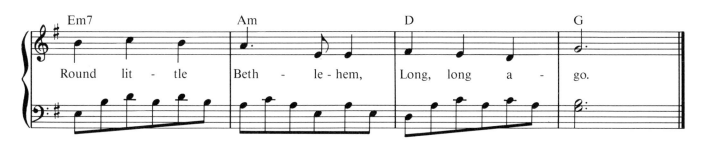

2 Sheep on the hillside lay
   Whiter than snow,
   Shepherds were watching them,
   Long, long ago.

3 Then from the starry skies
   Angels bent low,
   Singing their songs of joy,
   Long, long ago.

4 Wise men were following
   A star that did glow
   Far over Bethlehem,
   Long, long ago.

Suggestion

With extra verses added this carol can tell the
whole Nativity story and form the basis of a play.
Try making up a peaceful piece of instrumental
music to go in between the verses of this gentle
carol. Listen to the Pastoral Symphony from Han-
del's *Messiah*.

Accompaniment

Chime bars

Descant recorders

24
There was a pig

Narrative

In this song the farm animals take over the work on the farm on Christmas Day. Christmas is a time for being helpful to people.

The carol is called the Mummers' Carol. In the Middle Ages mummers were actors who mimed the actions of a song while someone sang it. (See also 'St George and the dragon', page 92.)

Traditional Lancashire children's carol,
arranged by Allen Percival

2　　There was a cow went out to plough, etc.

3　　There was a doe went out to hoe, etc.

4　　There was a drake went out to rake, etc.

5　　There was a crow went out to sow, etc.

6　　There was a sparrow went out to harrow, etc.

7　　There was a sheep went out to reap, etc.

8　　There was a minnow went out to winnow, etc.

9　　There was a cat who shook the mat, etc.

10　　There was a rook who was the cook, etc.

Suggestion

Make up a story about the animals helping the farmer and add more verses to the song. The song can be sung between the scenes of the play.

Something to think about

Can you think of other things that need doing that the animals might do? Talk about ways in which you can be especially helpful at Christmas time.

Accompaniment

Pitched percussion (Start with the voices)

25
The angel band

Narrative

A host of angels filled the sky. Their song was 'Peace on earth, goodwill to everyone'. Perhaps they danced as they sang. This lively Afro-American spiritual seems to skip along.

Words traditional
Music traditional,
Afro-American

Capo 1st fret
With vigour

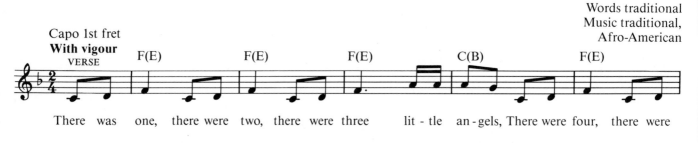

There was one, there were two, there were three lit-tle an-gels, There were four, there were

five, there were six lit-tle an-gels, There were se-ven, there were eight, there were nine lit-tle

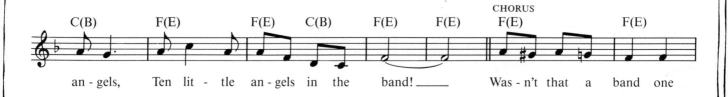

an-gels, Ten lit-tle an-gels in the band! ___ Was-n't that a band one

Sun-day mor-ning, Sun-day mor-ning, Sun-day mor-ning! Was-n't that a

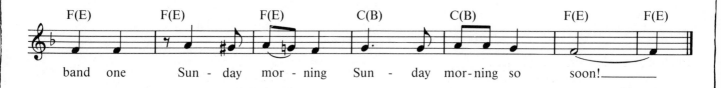

band one Sun-day mor-ning Sun-day mor-ning so soon! ___

Activity

With younger children make up a finger play. With older children create a dance in which the number of dancers gradually increases, or an instrumental piece in which ten instruments are introduced gradually.

The search for the baby

26   In the starlight
27   Go tell it on the mountain
28   Come, shepherds, come
29   Little star
30   Jesus loves us all
31   We are the Eastern kings
32   Men from the East
33   Follow the star
34   Joy all round (Koa, Koa, Koa)

26
In the starlight

Narrative

On the hillside the shepherds were afraid when the angels appeared. They were told to start their search for the new baby who was Christ the Lord.

Words traditional
Music traditional Czech

Lively

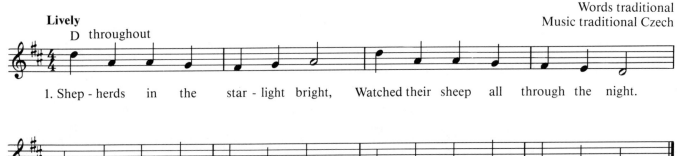

1. Shep - herds in the star - light bright, Watched their sheep all through the night.

Hi - dee, hi - day, hi - dee - um. Hi - dee, hi - day, hi - dee - um.

2 Angels singing said to them,
  'Hurry now to Bethlehem!'
  Hi-dee, hi-day, hi-dee-um,
  Hi-dee, hi-day, hi-dee-um!

3 'Christ, the holy babe is there,
  Lying in a manger bare.'
  Hi-dee, hi-day, hi-dee-um,
  Hi-dee, hi-day, hi-dee-um!

Accompaniment

Pitched percussion

Repeat throughout.

Suggestion

This song is based on one chord only. Follow it up by playing one chord only on chime bars or guitar and creating a new song.

27
Go tell it on the mountain

Narrative

Despite their fear the shepherds set out in their search. In this spiritual we are reminded that we too have to try hard to find the right things to do in life.

Capo 1st fret
With vigour

Words and music
traditional American

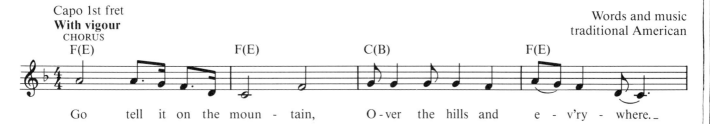

Go tell it on the moun - tain, O - ver the hills and e - v'ry - where.

Go tell it on the moun - tain That Je - sus Christ is born.

1. While shep - herds kept their watch - ing O'er wand' - ring flocks by night. Be -

hold from out the hea - vens, there shone a ho - ly light.

2 The shepherds feared and trembled
When, lo, above the earth
Rang out the angel chorus
That hailed our Saviour's birth.

CHORUS   Go tell it on the mountain, etc.

3 And lo, when they had seen it,
They all bowed down and prayed,
They travelled on together
To where the babe was laid.

CHORUS   Go tell it on the mountain, etc.

4 Down in a lowly manger
The blessed babe was born,
And God sent out salvation
Upon that blessed morn.

CHORUS   Go tell it on the mountain, etc.

5 And when I was a seeker,
I sought both night and day;
I asked the Lord to help me
And he showed me the way.

CHORUS   Go tell it on the mountain, etc.

Accompaniment

Use a drum in the rhythm ‖: ♩ ♪. ♪ ♩ ♩ :‖ to accompany this song.

28
Come, shepherds, come

Narrative

The shepherds arrive at the stable and decide to entertain the baby Jesus with singing, dancing and playing. They play the small hand drums commonly found in Middle Eastern countries. These are often made of pottery and are called *toft* or *dalbeke*. Do you think the baby Jesus enjoyed the music? It reminds us how the shepherds' search ended in happiness when they found the baby.

Words and music by
David Moses

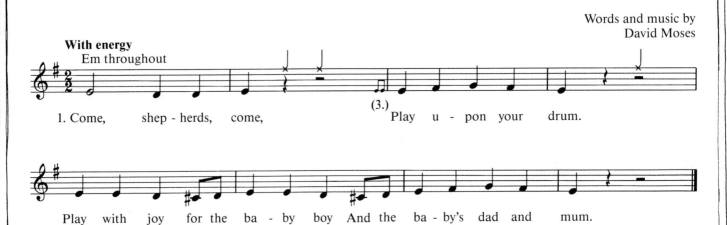

1. Come, shep - herds, come, (3.) Play u - pon your drum.

Play with joy for the ba - by boy And the ba - by's dad and mum.

2 Sing, shepherds, sing,

Sing for the new-born King,

Just a child, so meek and mild,

A little tiny thing.

3 Dance up and down

To the ricketty-racketty sound.

Listen to the beat and tap your feet;

Then wave your hands around.

52

Activity

Make up a dance for the shepherds.

Accompaniment

Use hand drums of the kind used in Middle Eastern
countries to accompany this song in one or all of
these rhythms. If pottery drums are not available,
bongos will do.

Hand drums

The 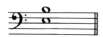 in the song can also be drumbeats or claps.

Bass instruments can play this throughout.

Bass instruments

29
Little star

Narrative

Far away in a country a long way from Bethlehem three Kings or Wise Men had studied the stars and consulted their books. Theirs was to be a long search, but they were sure that the star would guide them.

People have wondered a great deal about what the star was. Some say it was Halley's Comet, which, regular as clockwork once every 76 years, hurtles into the solar system to sweep through the night skies of planet Earth. It trails a fantastic fiery tail hundreds of thousands of kilometres long. Its last appearance was in 1986. Others think the star was a nova – a nova is an exploding star. It is also possible that two planets came so close that they appeared as one.

Today we know much more about space than in Jesus' day. People make complicated rockets to help in the exploration of space. They too make long journeys.

Words and music by
Cynthia Raza

Thoughtfully

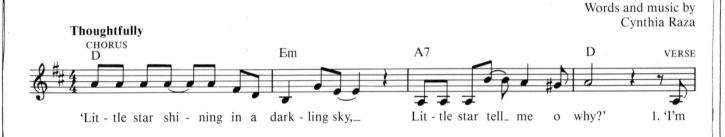

'Lit - tle star shi - ning in a dark - ling sky,_ Lit - tle star tell_ me o why?' 1. 'I'm

shi - ning on a mo-ther and her ba - by boy.'_ 'Lit - tle star now_ I know why.'

CHORUS 'Little star shining in a darkling sky', etc.

2 'I'm shining on the shepherds as they watch their sheep.'
'Little star now I know why.'

CHORUS 'Little star shining in a darkling sky', etc.

3 'I'm shining on the Wise Men as they come from afar.'
'Little star now I know why.'

CHORUS 'Little star shining in a darkling sky', etc.

4 'I'm shining on the children everywhere tonight.'
'Little star now I know why.'

Suggestion

With extra verses this carol can be used to tell the whole story from the star's point of view.

Accompaniment

Accompany this with bright-sounding metal instruments. You could use the rhythm throughout.

Lit - tle star

Recorders and pitched percussion

30
Jesus loves us all

Narrative

The kings did not set out empty handed. The rising of the star told them that the child they were looking for was also a king. Each of their gifts meant something: the gold was what kings wore, frankincense was burned in temples and showed that the child was God, and myrrh was a spice used in healing and showed that he was to suffer a great deal.

The kings are sometimes called the Magi. A Magus was a Wise Man, an astrologer, perhaps even a magician. Could these Wise Men see into the future? Is that why they chose the gifts of gold, frankincense and myrrh?

Words and music by
Cynthia Raza

2   Star led them to Bethlehem (*clap*, *clap*), my Lord.
     Star led them to Bethlehem (*clap*, *clap*), my Lord.
     Star led them to Bethlehem and Jesus loves us all;
     Jesus loves us all.

3   They brought gifts to Bethlehem, etc.

Alternative version

1   Baby born in Bethlehem (*clap, clap*), my Lord.
     Baby born in Bethlehem (*clap, clap*), my Lord.
     Baby born in Bethlehem and Jesus loves us all;
     Jesus loves us all.

2   Star shone over Bethlehem, etc.

3   Shepherds came to Bethlehem, etc.

4   Wise Men came to Bethlehem, etc.

Suggestion

This carol can be used to tell the whole story.

Accompaniment

The left hand of the piano and bass instruments can play 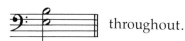 throughout.

This is a pentatonic tune using the scale E G A B D, and any accompaniment using these notes will work. Here are some examples:

OR

Repeat throughout.   Repeat throughout.

31
We are the Eastern kings

Narrative

Here the journey is difficult. The night is 'the darkest night there's ever been'. Perhaps the kings were often afraid, when robbers tried to steal their expensive gifts, or they were cold, tired and discouraged. But the star was always a ray of hope and eventually their journey ended in happiness.

Many people have set out on difficult journeys of exploration. They too were sometimes downhearted. Sometimes their journeys were successful, like the climbing of Mount Everest by Sir Edmund Hillary. Sometimes journeys ended in tragedy, like Captain Scott's expedition to Antarctica.

Words and music by
Irene Babsky

Driving forward

We are the East-ern kings Tra-v'ling o-ver the land,
Here on the de-sert sands, On the dark-est night there's e-ver been, oh yes!_ On the
dark-est night there's e-ver been, oh yes!_ On the dark-est night there's e-ver been.

2　We've journeyed very far,
　Over rivers and streams,

　　♪ ♩.
　Following the star,

　　♩ |
　The brightest star you've ever seen, oh yes!

　　♩ |
　The brightest star you've ever seen, oh yes!

　　♩ |
　The brightest star you've ever seen.

Suggestion

Follow this up with discussion about difficult journeys of exploration and discovery.

Accompaniment

Pitched percussion

You can add pitched percussion at the 'oh yes' playing:

Add maracas playing ‖: ♪♪ ♪♪ ♪♪ ♪♪ :‖

and claves ‖: ♩. ♩. ♩ :‖

Repeat them throughout.

32
Men from the East

Narrative

The Wise Men called on Herod to help them in their search. He told them where the Holy Book said that the Messiah would be born. He said that he too wanted to worship the baby, but he was lying. He told them to return to let him know the exact place, but the Wise Men had a dream warning them not to do this. So they set out for home a different way.

This carol also reminds us that we too set out on our journey in life to find God and happiness.

Words and music by
Geoffrey Ainger

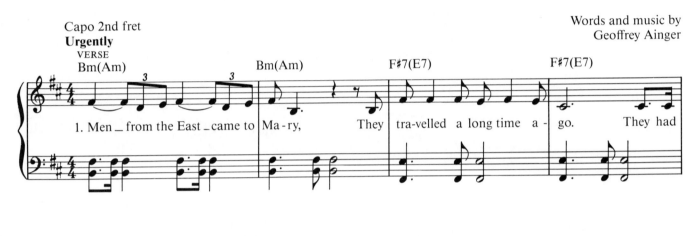

1. Men from the East came to Ma-ry, They tra-velled a long time a - go. They had

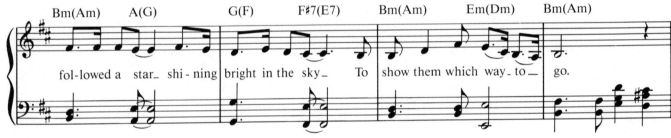

fol-lowed a star shi-ning bright in the sky To show them which way to go.

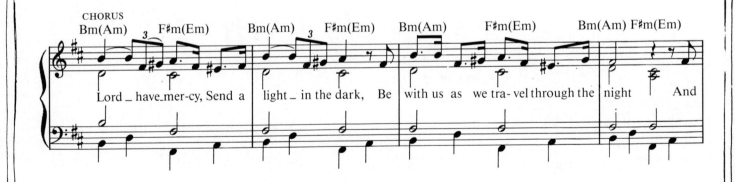

Lord have mer-cy, Send a light in the dark, Be with us as we tra-vel through the night And

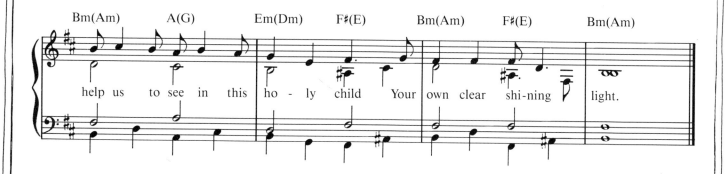

| Bm(Am) | A(G) | Em(Dm) | F♯(E) | Bm(Am) | F♯(E) | Bm(Am) |

help us to see in this ho - ly child Your own clear shi-ning light.

2 Men from the East came to Mary;
King Herod said 'You let me know,
If you come to that child
Born in Bethlehem town,
For I'd like to see him too.'

CHORUS   Lord have mercy, etc.

3 Men from the East came to Mary;
They offered their gifts to her son,
Then they travelled back home
By a different road
And not by the way they'd come.

CHORUS   Lord have mercy, etc.

4 We in our time come to Mary;
We may not have travelled so far,
But we're glad to be led
By the light of the truth
As those men were led by the star.

CHORUS   Lord have mercy, etc.

5 We in our time come to Mary;
We offer our gifts to her son
And our homage we pay
To the Saviour who made

A lowly stable his home.

CHORUS   Lord have mercy, etc.

Suggestion

Discuss ways in which Jesus can come today. Where can he be found?

Accompaniment

Chime bars
chorus only

33
Follow the star

Narrative

In this African carol the whole world seems to be called to follow the star. Imagine all the people and animals in the world journeying to the stable in Bethlehem following the star. What a procession!

Rich and poor people are still looking for Jesus today and many people try to visit Bethlehem. They especially want to see the church that now stands at the place where Jesus was born.

They enter the church through a small doorway and they have to bend down to get through it. It is rather like the doorway to the original cave. In the church they find a silver star set in the floor. These pilgrims find the same joy that the shepherds and kings found. We can share their joy as we look again at the scene around the manger.

African folksong
From *Folksongs of Africa*

2   Rise from your sleep, be gone ere the light of morning.

       CHORUS   This is the night, etc.

3   Come from the lakes and come from the flowing rivers.

       CHORUS   This is the night, etc.

4   Come from the hills and come from the lofty mountains.

       CHORUS   This is night, etc.

5   Come from the deserts, come from the growing forests.

       CHORUS   This is the night, etc.

6   Come from the towns and come from the busy cities.

       CHORUS   This is the night, etc.

7   Come from the plains and come from the fields of harvest.

       CHORUS   This is the night, etc.

8   Come from the swelling waters of all the oceans.

       CHORUS   This is the night, etc.

9   Follow the star that leads to the King of Glory.

       CHORUS   This is the night, etc.

Activity
Make a collage about all animals and people who come to worship Jesus.

Accompaniment
The timpani and conga parts are for adults to play and help to create an African sound.

34
Joy all round (Koa, Koa, Koa)

Narrative

In the stable by the manger many people found what they were looking for. Mary and Joseph had the joy of a new baby. The shepherds and kings found the baby they had been told about. This Maori song from New Zealand means 'Joy all round'. It is as if the whole world is caught up in the joy of Christmas.

Traditional Maori song

Koa   koa   koa   ha-ri   ta-ku   nga-kau   Koa   koa   koa   I   nga   wa   ka-

to - a   Ha-ri   ta-ku   nga-kau   Ki   to-nu   au   i-te   koa   koa   koa.

Activity

Make a happy collage of people enjoying themselves at the manger.

Accompaniment

The left hand of the keyboard and bass instruments can play:

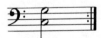

Repeat throughout.

Drums can play

Repeat throughout.

The journey to worship

35   Come, let us praise
36   A holy baby
37   Happy birthday
38   Carol of the drum
39   The orchestra carol
40   Carol of the birds

Bellbird

Brolga

Lorikeet

Bush-Martin

Friarbird

Pied Currawong

35
Come, let us praise

Narrative

Many carols call on people to praise the baby Jesus. Some people go on long journeys to holy places today to worship God. These journeys are called pilgrimages. Bethlehem is a favourite place for Christian pilgrims. Others go to Lourdes in France, for example, to be cured of their illnesses. Followers of religions other than Christianity also go on pilgrimages to their own holy places. Muslims, for example, try to go to Mecca in Saudi Arabia at least once in their lives. Hindus try to bathe in their holy river, the Ganges in India.

Words and music by
Punitha Perinparaja

Joyfully

Verses

1. & 3. Come let us praise sweet lit-tle babe. Come let us sing Hea-ven-ly King.

Mo-ther Ma-ry's ba-by Gent-ly smiles while sleep-ing. Eyes that

seek the glo-ry, Come and make your greet-ing. Hal-le-lu-ya, Hal-le-lu-

ya, Hal-le-lu-ya, Hal-le-lu-ya Hal-le-lu-ya, Hal-le-lu-

verse 1 | Last time | *Fine*

ya, Hal-le-lu-ya, Hal-le-lu-ya! Hal-le-lu-ya!

2. Fish-es of the deep sea, Stars that twin-kle so bright, Hills and lof-ty

moun-tains, Praise the won - der - ful sight. Peace on earth to bring Was born a

D.C. al fine

hea - ven - ly babe Joy - ful - ly let us sing To our new - born King.

Activity

Make a display of pictures of holy places surrounding a picture of a pilgrim in the centre.

Accompaniment

Accompany this by doubling the melody line on an instrument like an organ, harmonium or melodica. Make up instrumental interludes by repeating a phrase on the instrument alone. Play an Indian cymbal on the first beat of each bar. You could also add a drone on the left hand of a keyboard or other bass instrument.

36
A holy baby

Narrative

This carol from Africa asks us to look at the whole of Jesus' life so that we can understand that he is a special baby. It tells the story we have heard so far and how Mary and Joseph went on another long journey to safety in Egypt to escape Herod's anger.

When Herod died the family moved back to Nazareth, where Jesus grew up. Jesus was 12 years old when his parents made another trip, this time to Jerusalem, where he amazed the teachers in the temple with his intelligence. When he grew up, he went to the River Jordan and asked his cousin John the Baptist to baptise him. As he came up out of the water he saw the Spirit of God descending on him

like a bird and a voice from Heaven was heard saying, 'This is my Son, my Beloved.' He became famous as a preacher and a healer of the sick. He told people that God was his Father, and that God wanted everyone to love one another.

Jesus became too popular for the Jewish leaders, and they forced the Roman governor of their country to have him crucified, that is he was nailed to a wooden cross by his hands and feet and left to die. But Christians believe that he rose up from being dead because his body mysteriously vanished from its tomb. A few days later he appeared to some of his followers alive and well before he finally went up to Heaven to be with God, his Father.

Words by Tom Colvin
Music adapted from an
African tune

2   The simple shepherds soon left their sheep to search for him.

     CHORUS   He is Jesus, etc.

3   The Three Wise men came to offer gifts and worship him.

     CHORUS   He is Jesus, etc.

4   To Egypt land his parents flew from Herod's wrath.

     CHORUS   He is Jesus, etc.

5   He grew in wisdom in Nazareth of Galilee.

     CHORUS   He is Jesus, etc.

6   He taught the teachers in the temple of Jerusalem.

CHORUS   He is Jesus, etc.

7   In Jordan river the Holy Spirit came to him.

CHORUS   He is Jesus, etc.

8   He brought the Kingdom of Heaven to all believers.

CHORUS   He is Jesus, etc.

9   The sins of all men have nailed him to the Cross to die.

CHORUS   He is Jesus, etc.

10   God raised him up and brought him back to life again.

CHORUS   He is Jesus, etc.

11   He rose to Heaven to sit and rule at God's right hand.

CHORUS   He is Jesus, etc.

12   He is our Saviour and will stay with us evermore.

CHORUS   He is Jesus, etc.

Suggestion

Some people believe that soon after Jesus was crucified his very good friend, Joseph of Arimathea, came to England and planted his staff in Glastonbury in the County of Somerset. It grew roots and flowered, and is always in flower on January 6, one of the old dates of Christmas Day. Sprays of it are cut each year for the Queen's table on Christmas Day.

Legend also says that he buried the cup Jesus used at the Last Supper at Chalice Well in Glastonbury. This was the reason for one of the most famous searches in legend – King Arthur's search for the Holy Grail (the holy cup).

Many people still come to Glastonbury today on a pilgrimage to search for peace and joy in a holy place.

Make up a drama about Jesus coming to England with Joseph of Arimathea. Sing Blake's hymn 'And did those feet'.

37
Happy birthday

Narrative

A lot of people came to the stable to bring Jesus presents and wish him 'Happy birthday'. There are many stories of people who travelled long journeys to do this.

One is about a shepherd boy who took with him some wool to make the baby a pillow. On the way there he met a bird who needed material for its nest, so he gave some away. He also met a camel with a sore back and gave him some. Finally, he met a couple on a donkey who needed a soft saddle. He gave them the rest of the wool and told them his story.

Then he discovered that the man and his wife were Joseph and Mary on their way to Egypt with the baby Jesus. He was so happy that his search had ended in finding the baby he was looking for.

Words and music by
Jennifer Burnap

Happily

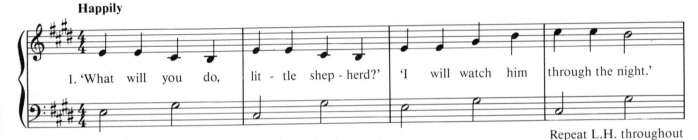

1. 'What will you do, lit - tle shep - herd?' 'I will watch him through the night.'

Repeat L.H. throughout

'What will you do, lit - tle star - let?' 'I will give to him my light.' 'What will you do?

What will you do? What will you do? What will you do?'_____

2   What will you do, little brown cow?'
     'I will give to him my hay.'
     'What will you do, little donkey?'
     'I will carry him some day.'

3   'What will you do, little children?'
     'We will sing for him a song.
     Happy birthday, little Jesus,
     We will sing it loud and long.'

4   'Happy birthday, happy birthday,
     Happy birthday is our song.
     Happy birthday, little Jesus,
     Happy birthday, loud and long.'

     CODA
     'What will you do?
     What will you do?
     What will you do?
     What will you do?'

Activity

Create a happy birthday dance for each to do for the baby Jesus.

Accompaniment

This song is based on the pentatonic scale:

Any accompaniment using these notes will fit, for example:

Choose a different instrument for each question.

38
Carol of the drum

Narrative

One legend says that there were originally four Wise Men searching for Jesus. The fourth was called Artaban and he sold his house for three jewels to give to the baby – a sapphire, a ruby and a pearl. He arranged to meet the three other Wise Men at a temple in Babylon. On the way he met a man ill by the roadside. He sold his sapphire so that the man could be looked after. But he wasted valuable time caring for the sick man. When he arrived at the temple the others had gone.

The same thing happened when he arrived at Bethlehem. Mary and Joseph and the baby Jesus had fled to Egypt and soldiers were killing baby boys on Herod's instructions. He gave the ruby to a soldier to save a baby from death.

For many years he searched for Jesus. He gave his last jewel, the pearl, to pay off the debts of a slave girl's father and save her from death, and this meant that he no longer had a gift for Jesus. Then one day he stood on the edge of a crowd to hear a man talking to the people. This is what he heard: 'Anything you do for one of my people here, however humble they are, you do for me.'

He thought of the gift he had tried to take to the baby in Bethlehem and realised that the man was, in fact, Jesus.

This song from Czechoslovakia tells of the offering of the little drummer boy to the baby. It shows how we can serve Jesus in all kinds of ways.

Traditional Czech,
arranged by Douglas Coombes

ra-pa-pa-pum, Ra-pa-pa-pum, Ra-pa-pa-pum. 'So to ho-nour him', Pa-

ra-pa-pa-pum, 'When we come.'

2   Baby Jesu, Pa-ra-pa-pa-pum,
    I am a poor boy too, Pa-ra-pa-pa-pum.
    I have no gift to bring, Pa-ra-pa-pa-pum.
    That's fit to give a king, Pa-ra-pa-pa-pum.
        Ra-pa-pa-pum, Ra-pa-pa-pum.
    Shall I play for you, Pa-ra-pa-pa-pum, On a drum?

3   Mary nodded, Pa-ra-pa-pa-pum,
    Ox and ass kept time, Pa-ra-pa-pa-pum.
    I played the drum for him, Pa-ra-pa-pa-pum.
    I played my best for him, Pa-ra-pa-pa-pum,
        Ra-pa-pa-pum, Ra-pa-pa-pum.

    Then he smiled at me, Pa-ra-pa-pa-pum, Me and my drum.

Suggestion

Invent a story that might be told before the carol is sung. Where did the little drummer boy come from? How did he learn to drum? How did the idea of playing for the baby come to him?

39
The orchestra carol

Narrative

There is a legend about an entertainer who travelled a great deal. One night he was a long way from his next stop and called at a monastery for shelter. He joined in the carols and went to sleep thinking of them. He felt sad that he could not join in this worship.

A little later the monks heard strange music coming from the chapel. The entertainer was surrounded by a mass of bottles, tins and different-shaped pieces of wood. They were all from the pack that he carried. He was making unusual but beautiful music by hitting them with two sticks.

Some of the monks wanted to stop him, but the Abbot smiled and explained to them that the man was praising God in the best way he could. He had found his own special way.

In this carol we are encouraged to praise God in *our* own way.

Words by Ann Mendoza and Pat Shaw
Music traditional Czech,
arranged by June Tillman

2   Strike up, Robert, on your bagpipe, etc.

   CHORUS   Come with me, etc.

3   Johnny, play on your recorder, etc.

   CHORUS   Come with me, etc.

4   Jenny, play on your triangle, etc.

   CHORUS   Come with me, etc.

5   Michael, join in with your fiddle, etc.

   CHORUS   Come with me, etc.

6   Sonia, play upon your side drum, etc.

   CHORUS   Come with me, etc.

Suggestion
Add as many verses as you like for the instruments you have available.

Accompaniment
Accompany each verse with an appropriate in-strument.

Pitched percussion

Repeat three times.

40
Carol of the birds

Narrative

This time of the birth of Jesus is thought to be very special. Animals and birds are said to do unusual things. Bees are said to hum the hundredth psalm in their hives at midnight. Animals speak amongst themselves; but it is dangerous to overhear them. Cows turn to the East. The cockerel is said to be the first to tell of Jesus' birth by crowing 'Christus natus est.' This means 'Christ is born' in Latin. So cocks crow on Christmas Eve and even weathercocks join them.

In this carol from Australia, birds join in praising the newborn baby. The brolgas are thin graceful birds rather like flamingos. They do a very beautiful dance to attract their mates. The bell-birds live in rain forests and get their name from the bell-like sound that they make. Currawongs and lorikeets are members of the parrot family. 'Orana' means 'Welcome'. It is a word used by the Aborigines who live in Australia.

Words by John Wheeler
Music by William G. James

Brightly

1. Out on the plains the brol-gas are danc-ing, Lift-ing their feet like war-hor-ses pranc-ing: Up to the sun the wood-larks go wing - ing Faint in the dawn light e-choes their sing-ing-'O-ra - na! O - ra - na! O - ra-na! To Christ-mas Day.'

2 Down where the tree-ferns grow by the river,
There where the waters sparkle and quiver,
Deep in the gullies bell-birds are chiming,

Softly and sweetly their lyric notes rhyming –
'Orana! Orana! Orana! To Christmas Day.'

3 Friar-birds sip the nectar of flowers,
Currawongs chant in wattle-tree bowers;
In the blue ranges lorikeets calling –
Carols of bushbirds rising and falling –
'Orana! Orana! Orana! To Christmas Day.'

Giving presents

41   Bom, bom, bom!
42   Giving and getting
43   Christmas is coming
44   Come a see Jesus
45   In the stable
46   Enjoying Christmas
47   I have got a Christmas gift

41
Bom, bom, bom!

Narrative

What present would you want to give the baby Jesus? Would you bring him food, a toy, clothes, or play an instrument for him? In many parts of the world people still leave presents for the poor at a crib. Some of the Puerto Rican community in New York dress up as the kings on the 6th of January and go round homes giving out fruit and nuts.

Traditional Chilean,
arranged by June Tillman

La-dy Ma - ry, La-dy Ma - ry, Bom, bom, bom! I have shoes for ba - by

Je - sus, Bom, bom, bom! Lit - tle shoes I hope will please him, Bom,

bom, bom! Lit - tle crim - son za - pa - ti - tos, Bom, bom, bom!

2 Lady Mary, Lady Mary,
     Bom, bom, bom!
   I have come across the city,
     Bom, bom, bom!
   Come to see the holy figures,
     Bom, bom, bom!
   In the manger hushed and pretty,
     Bom, bom, bom!

3 Lady Mary, Lady Mary,
     Bom, bom, bom!
   There's a mouse inside the manger,
     Bom, bom, bom!
   See, he's nibbling at the donkey,
     Bom, bom, bom!
   Do you like the little stranger?
     Bom, bom, bom!

Original Spanish

1 Señora doña María,
     Bom, bom, bom!
   yo vengo del otro lado,
     Bom, bom, bom!
   yal niño Jesus le traigo,
     Bom, bom, bom!
   zapatito colorado,
     Bom, bom, bom!

2 En el portal de Belén.
     Bom, bom, bom!
   hay un nido de ratones,
     Bom, bom, bom!
   y al patriarca San José,
     Bom, bom, bom!
   le han comido los calzones,
     Bom, bom, bom!

Suggestion

Use 'bom, bom, bom!' as the basis for a piece.
Make up a recorder tune to go with it.

Accompaniment

Xylophone

Repeat throughout. Add a drum on the 'bom, bom,
bom!'.

42
Giving and getting

Narrative

Long before Christians started celebrating Christmas, the Romans celebrated the festival of Saturnalia around the 25th of December. For seven days they feasted to celebrate the passing of the shortest and darkest day of the year, which meant being able to look forward to the sun and warmth again. Ordinary life was turned upside down – slaves were set free for seven days, masters waited at table, all work stopped, and everyone ate and drank too much. Exchanging presents was an important part of this festival, and Christians borrowed the custom.

Jesus was God's gift to the world, so that is why we still give gifts today.

The three Wise Men brought gifts to Jesus. The sixth of January is the day when we remember the Wise Men especially. We call it the feast of Epiphany. On that day two gentleman ushers represent the Queen at a service in the Chapel Royal. They offer gold (25 gold sovereigns), frankincense and myrrh: the twenty-five gold sovereigns are given to the poor and old; the frankincense is given to the church to be burned at services; the myrrh, a soothing ointment, is given to a hospital.

Words and music by
David Moses

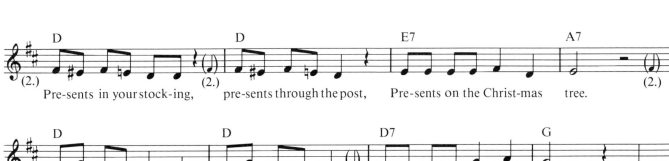

Pre-sents in your stock-ing, pre-sents through the post, Pre-sents on the Christ-mas tree.

Tear-ing off the pa - per, yel-low, red and gold, Pur-ple, pink and green and blue, I'm

sure you all be-lieve it is love-ly to re-ceive, But it's lots of fun to give things too. ____

CHORUS   Give a little joy, etc.

2   Choosing soap for Mum, the chemist's shop is fun

With soap of every colour, shape and smell.

A pair of socks for Dad, the best he's ever had,

Don't they seem to fit him well.

I've bought my sister Flo a doll that says 'Hello';

I've put it in a secret hiding-place.

I only hope I can afford some hankies for my Gran,

'Cause I love to see the smile upon her face.

CHORUS   Give a little joy, etc.

Something to think about

The song says that giving presents brings more happiness than receiving them. Do you think that this is true?

Activity

Make a collage of Christmas presents of various shapes and sizes.

43
Christmas is coming

Narrative

Christmas is a time to give to people less well-off than ourselves. Boxing Day was the traditional time for giving. Many churches have boxes in which you can put money for poor people. In the Middle Ages priests opened these boxes on the day after Christmas. Later wealthy people gave servants gifts of money in small boxes called 'Christmas Boxes'.

Today we give presents to people who serve us during the year – the postman and the dustman, for example. We usually give them before Christmas.

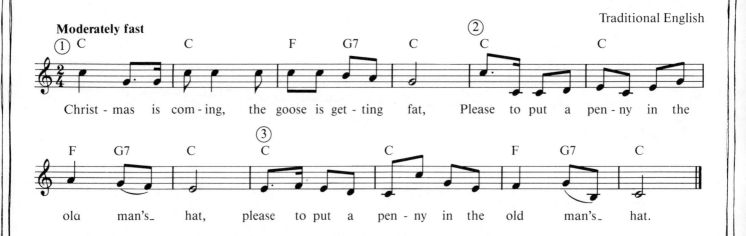

This is a round. Other voices enter at marked points.

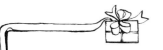

Something to think about

Can you also think of a poor person or an organisation that helps poor people? Could you give them some money this Christmas? Look for ways of helping the poor. Perhaps you could arrange a special party for them.

Activity

Mime a scene of an old man on the pavement and various people passing by. Or create a tableau with life-size cut-outs of children in the class.

Accompaniment

These patterns on pitched percussion:

Repeat each throughout.

Recorders

Repeat throughout.

44
Come a see Jesus

Narrative

There is so much to do at Christmas. It is a time for sending cards, and a time for parties. It is a time for getting and giving presents. Amidst all this we sometimes forget that gifts are given to remind us of God's gift of His Son to us. We must always remember to say thank you to people who give us presents.

Words and music by
David Moses

85

CHORUS   Christmas, what a dis Christmas, etc.?

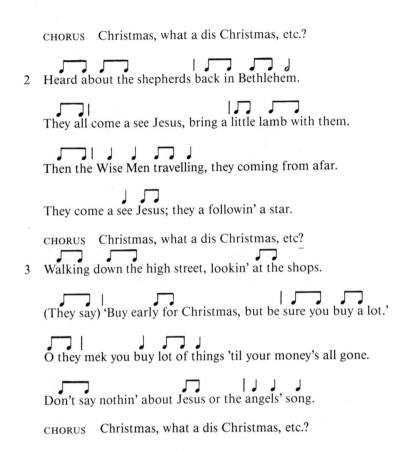

2 Heard about the shepherds back in Bethlehem.

They all come a see Jesus, bring a little lamb with them.

Then the Wise Men travelling, they coming from afar.

They come a see Jesus; they a followin' a star.

CHORUS   Christmas, what a dis Christmas, etc?

3 Walking down the high street, lookin' at the shops.

(They say) 'Buy early for Christmas, but be sure you buy a lot.'

O they mek you buy lot of things 'til your money's all gone.

Don't say nothin' about Jesus or the angels' song.

CHORUS   Christmas, what a dis Christmas, etc.?

Something to think about

Have you ever thought of thanking God for his gifts? Imagine what it would be like to be deaf. Then try thinking of all the things you would miss – birds, friends' voices, singing. Thank God for his gift of hearing. Are there other things that you can be thankful for?

Suggestion

Make a list of all the things you could say thank you to God for.

45
In the stable

Narrative

There is a story about a little boy from a poor family. His mother could not afford a present, but gave her son a kiss. They talked of the joy of Christmas. As the boy hung up his stocking she said that God would fill it with the best gift of all, the gift that you cannot see.

In the morning he awoke happily. He clutched his empty stocking and ran through the streets crying: 'My stocking is full of the best gift of all, the gift I cannot see.'

The grim mayor was filled with joy by the boy's happiness. That night he went to the house with a basket of gold pieces. He asked the mother to accept them because her son had shared with him the best gift of all.

This song talks about the value of the gift of love.

Words by Hilda Rostron
Music by Colin Peters

The shep-herds found the sta-ble And saw the ba-by there; They quiet-ly knelt be-side him And said a 'thank-you' prayer.

2   The Wise Men found the baby
      And gave gifts, one, two, three;
   Today it is his birthday . . .
      My gift is – love from me.

Suggestion

This song uses only four notes. Use either these or another four notes to make a new tune.

Accompaniment

Add an Indian cymbal on the first and third beats of each bar.

Pitched percussion

46
Enjoying Christmas

Narrative

Have you noticed how the Christmas tree fills all the room with the smell of pine? Feel how smooth and round the coloured balls that decorate it are. Feel the prickly needles of the Christmas tree. Listen to the sound of the bells on the cuddly toys that we give as presents. Listen to the songs of the carol singers. Be thankful for the gift of all our senses that help us enjoy the world so much.

Words by June Tillman
Music traditional,
adapted by June Tillman

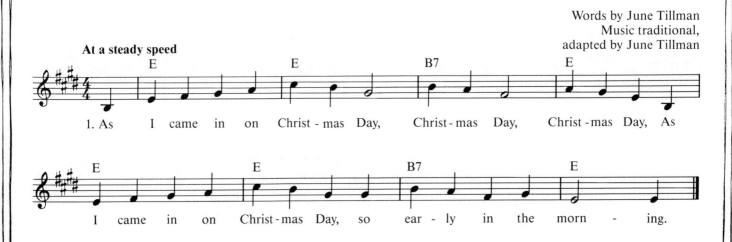

At a steady speed

1. As I came in on Christ-mas Day, Christ-mas Day, Christ-mas Day, As
I came in on Christ-mas Day, so ear-ly in the morn - ing.

2 I smelt the pine on Christmas Day, Christmas Day, Christmas Day,
I smelt the pine on Christmas Day, so early in the morning.

3 I felt the smooth and shiny bell, shiny bell, shiny bell,
I felt the smooth and shiny bell, so early in the morning.

4 I felt the prickle of the leaves, etc.

5 I heard the bells ring loud and clear, etc.

6 I heard the crispy crunch of snow, etc.

7 I tasted nuts and fruits so sweet, etc.

8 I saw the coloured lights that flash, etc.

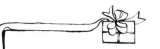

Alternative version

1 As I went over Bethl'em Hill, Bethl'em Hill, Bethl'em Hill,
   As I went over Bethl'em Hill, so early in the morning.

2 I clapped my hands on Bethl'em Hill, etc.

3 I stamped my feet on Bethl'em Hill, etc.

4 I jumped for joy on Bethl'em Hill, etc.

Something to think about

We use our eyes so much. Have you ever thought
of all the things we don't see that we can enjoy at
Christmas? Imagine what it would be like to be
blind at Christmas.

Suggestion

This song can be adapted to include many aspects
of Christmas.

Accompaniment

Use a tambourine in the rhythm

Repeat throughout.

Christ-mas Day

Pitched percussion

47
I have got a Christmas gift

Narrative

Some people like unwrapping best of all. Have you ever listened to the sound that various types of paper make? Listen to the soft sound of tissue paper, the rattle of foil and the crackle of brown paper as you unwrap your presents this Christmas.

Presents sometimes have a special meaning. To the Chinese the colour red means wealth and good fortune, so at Chinese New Year children are often given red envelopes containing presents of money.

In Scotland and the North of England at New Year the first person to come into a home on New Year's Day is called a 'first footer'. First footers carry bread, salt and coal, which means that the house will have food, wealth and warmth in the New Year. In return, first footers should be offered a drink and a kind of cake called 'black bun'.

Words and music by
Monica Shelton

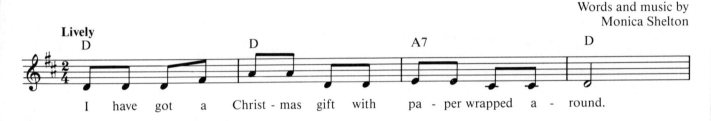

I have got a Christ - mas gift with pa - per wrapped a - round.

When I take the pa - per off it, li - sten to the sound.

Activity

Make up a piece of music based on paper rustles of different kinds.

Accompaniment

Accompany this song with rustles of as many different types of paper as you can.

Plays, carols and cribs

48 St George and the dragon
49 Cornish wassail
50 Letter carol
51 Gatatumba
52 Oh, how wondrous

48
St George and the dragon

Narrative

Christmas is traditionally a time for plays. Mummers were ordinary people who dressed up and went from house to house acting, miming and dancing. They were rewarded with food and drink. Their plays told stories of life winning over death and evil defeated by good.

One of the most popular stories was 'St George and the Dragon'. In this play St George was killed by the Turkish knight and brought back to life by the doctor.

Pantomimes have been popular in England for over 200 years. The stories are nearly always taken from fairy tales and nursery rhymes like 'Cinderella' and 'The Babes in the Wood'. In these, too, good wins over evil. Over the years pantomimes have got grander, with magnificent scenery and costumes and many different acts.

Words and music by
June Tillman

Capo 1st fret
With vigour

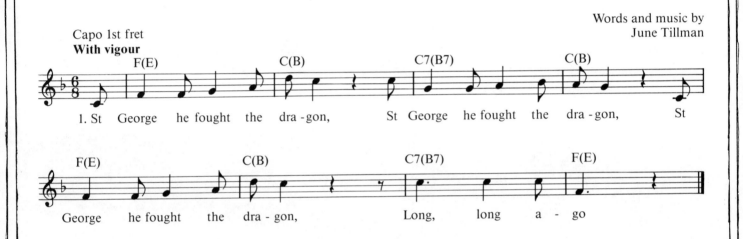

1. St George he fought the dra-gon, St George he fought the dra-gon, St George he fought the dra-gon, Long, long a-go

2 He saved the lovely princess, etc.

3 The Turkish knight he slew him, etc.

4 The doctor came and saved him, etc.

5 St George he wed the princess, etc.

6 And now they both are happy, etc.

Suggestion

This song can be adapted for any story you wish.

Alternative version: Cinderella

1 Cinderella's in the kitchen,

   Cinderella's in the kitchen,

   Cinderella's in the kitchen,

   Long, long ago.

2 She's sad among the cinders, etc.

3 She's left out of the ball, etc.

4 A fairy comes to see her, etc.

5 She grants her every wish, etc.

6 She goes off to the ball, etc.

7 She dances with the prince, etc.

8 When midnight strikes she leaves, etc.

9 She leaves her shoe behind her, etc.

10 The prince comes looking for her, etc.

11 The slipper fits her foot, etc.

12 She weds the handsome prince, etc.

13 And now they both are happy, etc.

Accompaniment

Use drums in the rhythm

Pitched percussion

49
Cornish wassail

Narrative

Wassailing traditionally took place on Twelfth Night, the evening of the twelfth day after Christmas. The 'wassail' cup was a hot drink made of cloves, ginger, nutmeg, sugar, eggs, apple and ale. It was served from huge silver or pewter bowls. Farmers went into the fields and sprinkled apple trees with the mixture, hoping to encourage a good crop next year. In other areas groups of wassailers went from house to house asking for money in return for good luck.

In some places that still follow the tradition of wassailing a horse's head on a long stick is carried by one of the wassailers. Its body is covered with a white sheet and its jaws can be made to open and shut.

Traditional English

1. Now Christ - mas is come. The New Year be - gin, Pray o - pen your door _ and let us come in. To our _ war - zail, war - zail, war - zail And joy _ come to _ our jol - ly war - zail.

2 Here at your door, already stand,

The jolly warzail boys with a bowl in our hand.

CHORUS To our warzail, etc.

3 Good master and mistress sitting down at your ease,

Put your hand in your pocket, and give what you please.

CHORUS To our warzail, etc.

4   This ancient old house we will kindly salute,

It is an old custom you need not dispute.

CHORUS   To our warzail, etc.

5   We wish you a blessing and a long life to live

Since you've been so free and so willing to give.

CHORUS   To our warzail, etc.

6   The saddle and bridle lie upon the shelf

If you want any more you must sing it yourself.

CHORUS   To our warzail, etc.

Activity

Get a big wassail bowl and make a special mix of
fruit juices and different flavourings.

Accompaniment

Pitched percussion

Recorders

50
Letter carol

Narrative

A carol is a song of joy and happiness. A long time ago people danced to carols as well as singing them. Hymns in church in those days were in Latin; but these carols were in the language that ordinary people spoke and could understand. They were sung in the halls of rich people and then by singers going from house to house. Carol-singers help people feel cheerful at Christmas time.

Words and music by
Ian Sharp

Capo 1st fret
Brightly

1.C is for the

Crib where the Christ child lay in the sta - ble at Beth - le - hem:

Sing we a ca - rol to the Lord. Lord.

2   A is for the Angels who sang of his birth to humble working men:

CHORUS   Sing we a carol to the Lord.

3   R is for the Road the Wise Men trod as they travelled through the night:

CHORUS   Sing we a carol to the Lord.

4   O is for the Offering we all prepare for Christ, our Shepherd King:

CHORUS   Sing we a carol to the Lord.

5   L is for the Love we give away to those we meet each day:

CHORUS   Sing we a carol to the Lord.

6   Carol it to me, and Carol it to you, and Carol it across the sea:

CHORUS   Sing we a carol to the Lord.

Suggestion

Create a dance to go with this carol. It could be a
circle dance with people holding up the letters
mentioned.

Try adding clapping and unpitched percussion to
the chorus. The verses could be sung by a soloist or
by a small group.

51
Gatatumba

Narrative

Some carols have interesting stories behind them. Just before Christmas in 1818 the church as Obendorf in Austria faced a crisis. The organ wouldn't work, and it was discovered that mice had been gnawing holes in the bellows. The pastor, Joseph Mohr, and the organist, Franz Grüber, got together and wrote a new carol. It could be accompanied by a guitar and did not need the organ, so the people could sing it on Christmas morning. That carol was the beautiful 'Silent Night'. So their search for a way to get round a difficulty gave us a lovely carol.

In 1745 a certain Dr Byrom searched for a new and different present for his daughter. He succeeded when he wrote 'Christians awake! Salute the happy morn'.

This lively carol from Spain calls on us to bring all our instruments to praise the new baby.

Words by Ann Mendoza
Music traditional Spanish,
arranged by June Tillman

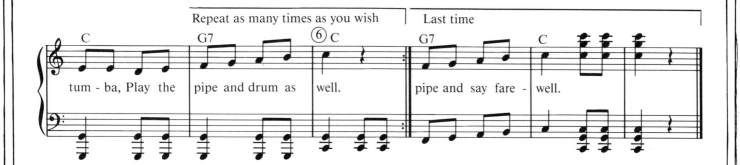

Repeat as many times as you wish | Last time

C   G7   ⑥ C   G7   C

tum - ba, Play the | pipe and drum as | well.   : | pipe and say fare - | well.

Something to think about

Do you think Dr Byrom's daughter was pleased with her carol? Can you think of any special presents you have received? Can you think of any special ones you might make for people?

Accompaniment

Play a guiro during the introduction on the first beat of each bar. At figure 2 add maracas playing

At 3 add tambourines in the rhythm of the left hand. At 4 add a bell on the first beat of the bar. At 5 add a drum in the rhythm of the left hand. Let a recorder play the last C at 6.

Suggestion

Make up a piece in which the instruments are added one after the other.

52

Oh, how wondrous

Narrative

In 1224, St Francis of Assisi searched for a way to help people to understand what the first Christmas would have been like. At Graecia in Italy he arranged a real live scene with real people and a real ox and ass around a manger. He held a service and talked about the birth of a poor baby.

This was the first crib. Now, a crib is usually a group of statues representing people and animals in the Christmas story. This custom probably dates from the time when the Romans became Christians and made dolls that looked like Mary, Joseph and Jesus, and sold them in the streets of Rome.

Many people have tried to find out what the first Christmas was like by looking at a crib in school, home or church. Sing this carol from Poland looking at the crib scene.

Words translated by Beryl Tučapská
Music: Czech carol,
arranged by Antonín Tučapský

At moderate speed and in smooth singing style

1. Oh, how won - drous

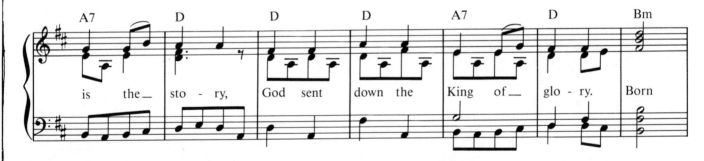

is the _ sto - ry, God sent down the King of _ glo - ry. Born

in a sta - ble _ here; in truth our lives to share.

2 There he lies in manger lowly, Jesus Christ our King most holy.
  Born all our hearts to win and save us all from sin.

3 What can we poor children bring him? We have nought of worth to give him.
  We'll sing a happy song and cheer his day along.

Decorations
and cards

53   I saw three ships
54   I am a pine tree
55   In forests dark
56   The whole world is a Christmas tree
57   Carol for Christingle
58   Silver and gold
59   Jesus was a baby
60   Winter things

53
I saw three ships

Narrative

Long before Jesus was born, evergreens were carried into houses as a symbol of everlasting life. They were green and living when all other plants seemed dead. In Northern Europe people believed that woodland spirits lived in them. In Italy, the evergreens were in honour of Saturn, the god of growing things. Mistletoe, holly and ivy had a special place in pagan worship because they had berries in winter when other trees were bare. So these trees have both a pagan and a Christian meaning.

The holly was special to many people including the Druids, the Persians and the Chinese. The North-American Indians planted it round their huts to protect them from evil spirits and used it to treat measles. Holly hung up in barns in England was thought to make animals healthy. It is supposed to be unlucky to leave holly up after Twelfth Night, and it must all be burned, not thrown away. People used to see it as a sign of peace and health. For Christians it represents the crown of thorns that Jesus wore when he was killed. It is said that the berries were originally yellow, but were stained red by his blood.

Ivy was used for curing ulcers and corns. It was used to foretell the future. An ivy leaf was placed in a bowl of water from New Year's Eve to Twelfth Night. If it remained green, the next year would be happy. Worn on the head, ivy was thought to prevent baldness. On the walls of houses, it was said to protect people against witches. If a woman walked through a field with ivy in her pocket, the first man she met she would marry.

Mistletoe has a great number of stories told about it. It was used to cure any illness from the common cold to the bite of a mad dog. African warriors carried it to protect them from being hurt. In Wales it was said that if you put mistletoe under your pillow you would see the future.

Another legend tells of Baldur, the Norse sun god. He was so fine that the other gods promised not to hurt him. A spell was placed on everything so that nothing would harm him, but he forgot the mistletoe. Loki, the god of evil, made a sharp arrow out of a mistletoe branch. He guided blind Höder's hand to fire it and kill Baldur. The other gods brought him back to life and the mistletoe promised never to hurt anyone again. In another legend it was the wood used to make the cross on which Jesus was killed. It was so ashamed of this that it shrank from being a tree to being a plant that can only exist on other trees.

Other evergreens were also part of Christmas. Laurel was used in decorating. The herb rosemary decorated the boar's head which was traditionally eaten at Christmas. In many countries people hang a wreath of evergreens on their doors at Christmas. Evergreens have always been part of people's search for hope in the midst of winter.

Traditional British

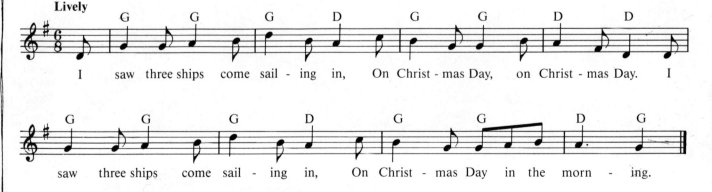

2 And what do you think was in them then,
   On Christmas Day, on Christmas Day?

   And what do you think was in them then,
   On Christmas Day in the morning?

3 Some pine branches and holly boughs, etc.

4 Some ivy and some mistletoe, etc.

5 Some laurel and some rosemary, etc.

Extra verses

6 A Christmas tree and coloured lights, etc.

7 A paper chain and shining balls, etc.

8 A crib with ox and ass so poor, etc.

9 A carol we can dance and sing, etc.

10 A robin on a Christmas card, etc.

11 Some presents for you and me to give, etc.

12 Some pantomimes and circuses, etc.

13 And love and joy was in those ships, etc.

14 And all the bells on earth shall ring, etc.

15 And all the angels in heaven shall sing, etc.

Suggestion

You can add the religious verses if you wish. Use whichever verses are suitable for your pageant. The carol could accompany a procession of 'ships' containing all these Christmas customs.

Accompaniment

Recorders

Pitched percussion

Repeat throughout starting on the first beat of the bar

54

I am a pine tree

Narrative

The oak tree was worshipped by pagan people. A German legend tells how St Boniface was sent from England to Germany to tell people about Jesus. He came across a group of people worshipping a pagan god under an oak. They were about to kill a boy as a sacrifice to the god. As they led the boy forward St Boniface cut down the oak. As it fell, it left behind a little fir tree growing between its roots. The saint said that from then on the fir tree would be a sign of peace and everlasting life. It would point to heaven and remind people of the Christ child, and this is why we now use fir trees as Christmas trees.

Words and music by
Louise B. Scott

Capo 1st fret

Swaying

I am a pine tree stand-ing on a hill. I can stand so ve-ry, ve-ry still.

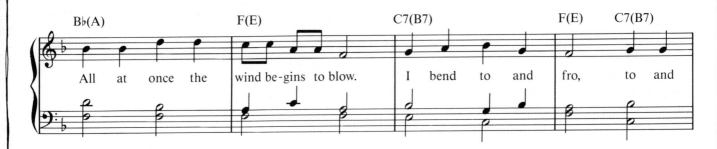

All at once the wind be-gins to blow. I bend to and fro, to and

fro, to and fro.

Coda for swaying

Use green scarves as you sway about.

55
In forests dark

Narrative

Long before people set up Christmas trees they used to make a Kissing Bough. This was a hoop covered in evergreens. Candles were fastened on it, and apples, ornaments, small gifts and mistletoe were hung from it. It was the most important decoration in the room, just as the Christmas tree is today. So, how did the custom of the Christmas tree come about?

Well, it was really Queen Victoria's husband, Prince Albert, who first introduced the Christmas tree into Britain about 150 years ago. He was a German prince and he brought the custom from Germany.

Every year since 1946 Norway has sent Britain a gift of a huge tree to stand in Trafalgar Square in London. This is their way of thanking the British people for their help during the Second World War.

Words by B. Charlesworth
Music by H. Bates

At a moderate speed

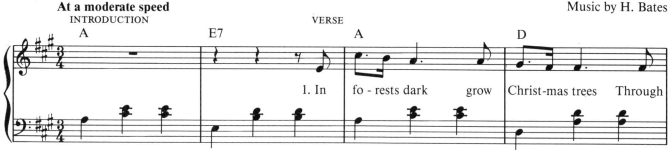

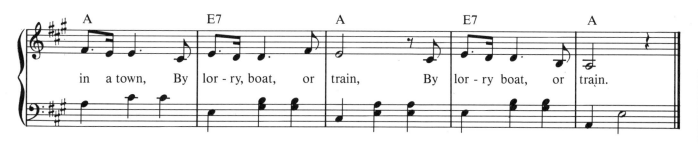

2   The trees we have at Christmas time
Are fir trees tall and evergreen.
And when they're hung with many toys
By happy laughing girls and boys
They brighten any scene,
They brighten any scene.

3   On every sloping branch there hang
With merriment and laughing song
Some chocolate shapes and fairy lights,
Some stars and globes and tinsel bright,
When Christmas comes along,
When Christmas comes along.

56
The whole world is a Christmas tree

Narrative

One night Martin Luther saw the stars shining through the branches of a fir tree. He went home and decorated his tree with candles to remind people of the starry heaven from which Christ would come.

Candles play an important part in the Christmas search for Christ, the Light of the World. In Sweden the 13th of December is the feast day of St Lucia. She was a Christian killed for her faith in Italy. On this day early in the morning, the youngest daughter of the family dresses in white. She places on her head an evergreen wreath with seven lighted candles. She brings coffee and 'Lucia cats'. These are little buns in the shape of a cat's head. She serves them to the other members of the family in their bedrooms.

Many religions use lights at important festivals. Hindus light little lights at Diwali, the New Year Hindu festival. Jews light candles at Hanukka when they celebrate the rebuilding of the temple.

Words by Arthus Leon Moore
Music traditional American

With dignity

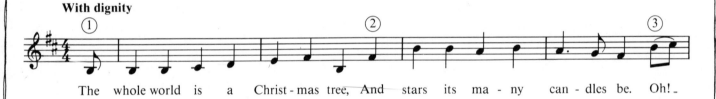

The whole world is a Christ-mas tree, And stars its ma-ny can-dles be. Oh!_

Sing a ca-rol joy-ful-ly, The_ year's great_ feast is keep-ing.

Accompaniment

Accompany this with bright metal instruments such as triangles.

57
Carol for Christingle

Narrative

Christingle is a pretty custom from Czechoslova-kia. At a service children are given an orange with a candle, four feathers and sweets stuck in it. This carol tells us all about this custom.

Words by Fred Pratt Green
Music traditional Czech, arranged by June Tillman

Lively but not too fast

1. O round as the world is the o - range you give us! And hap - py are they who to Je - sus be - long. So let the world know as you join in Christ - in - gle, That Je - sus, the Hope of the World, is our song.

2 O bright is the flame of the candle you give us!
And happy are they who to Jesus belong:
So let the world know, as we join in Christingle,
That Jesus, the Light of the World, is our Song.

3 Go northward or southward, go eastward or westward,
How happy are they who to Jesus belong:
So let the world know, as we join in Christingle,
That Jesus, the Peace of the World, is our song.

4 When homeward we go, we must take Jesus with us,
For happy are we who to Jesus belong;
So let the world know, as we join in Christingle,
That Jesus, the Saviour of All, is our Song.

58
Silver and gold

Narrative

For people living in cities it is difficult to find evergreens such as holly and ivy; they have to think of other ways of making their cribs look attractive. Italians like to use cloth and paper.

When it became easy to cut paper with machines in the nineteenth century, paper decorations became common.

There is an interesting decoration found in Sweden and Italy. In Italy it is called a *ceppo* and in Sweden a *julhög*. It is a combination of a crib and a Christmas tree, a wooden triangle with candles along its sides and three shelves. One carries fruit, one presents and one a crib scene.

This carol tells us how the colours of our decorations can remind us of parts of the Christmas story.

Words and music by
Cynthia Raza

With feeling

1. Sil - ver snow, Sil - ver light, Ba - by born on a si - lent night. It's Christ - mas. Ring out the bells and sing out the song, Ring out the bells and sing out the song, Ring a ding, ring a ding dong.

2 Golden crowns,
Golden stars,

Kings are coming from afar.

CHORUS   It's Christmas, etc.

3 White and soft,
White and still,

Lambs are born, Shepherds watch on the hill.

CHORUS   It's Christmas, etc.

Activity

Draw coloured patterns using only the colours mentioned in the song.

Accompaniment

Choose a different instrument for each colour and accompany the verses. Use bells for the chorus.

Recorders

Pitched percussion (or easier descant recorder)

59
Jesus was a baby

Narrative

The robin is often found on Christmas cards. One legend tells how he got his red breast by fanning the flames of the fire in the stable in Bethlehem to keep Jesus warm. Another legend says that he got it by taking out thorns from Jesus' head when he was being killed. This carol describes the traditional nativity scene pictured on so many Christmas cards.

Capo 3rd fret
Gospel rock

Words and music by
David Moses

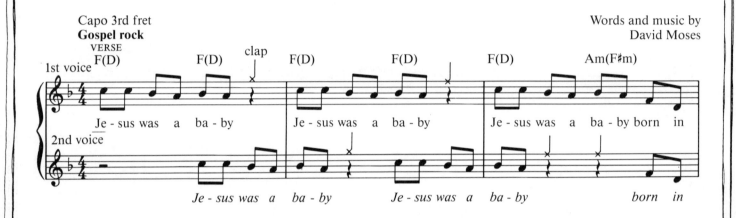

1st voice: Je-sus was a ba-by / Je-sus was a ba-by / Je-sus was a ba-by born in

2nd voice: Je-sus was a ba-by / Je-sus was a ba-by / born in

Beth - le - hem._ / Ma - ry was his mam-ma / Mary was his mam-ma

Beth - le - hem._ / Ma - ry was his mamma / Ma - ry was his

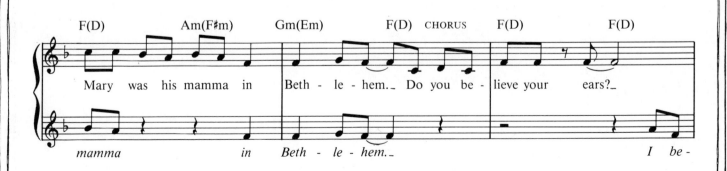

Mary was his mamma in / Beth - le - hem._ Do you be - lieve your ears?_

mamma in Beth - le - hem._ / I be-

110

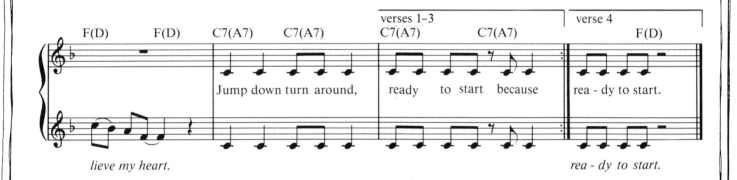

2 Joseph was his daddy, Joseph was his daddy, Joseph was his daddy
   In Bethlehem.
   Shepherds came to see him, shepherds came to see him, shepherds came to see him
   In Bethlehem.

   CHORUS   Do you believe your ears, etc.

3 Angels singing glory, etc.
   Telling out the story, etc.

   CHORUS   Do you believe your ears, etc.

4 Fire burning dimly, etc.
   Robin gently fanned it, etc.

   CHORUS   Do you believe your ears, etc.

Activity

Collect as many versions of the crib scene as you
can and make a collage of them.

60
Winter things

Narrative

We all like getting Christmas cards. They help us to feel that we belong to a family or have lots of friends. Christmas cards became common in the last century, when the post began. This meant that people could send cards cheaply to their friends. Many of the pictures you see on cards are described in this song. Even in countries where it is summer at Christmas, the same pictures are found on cards.

Words and music by
Cynthia Raza

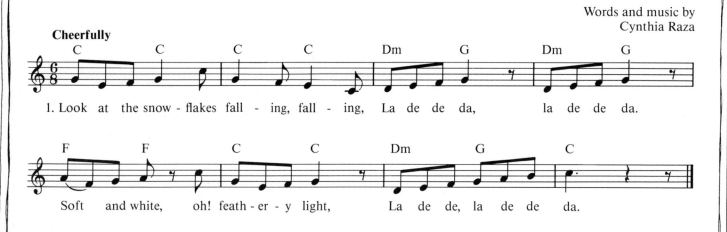

1. Look at the snow-flakes fall - ing, fall - ing, La de de da, la de de da.

Soft and white, oh! feath-er-y light, La de de, la de de da.

2   Look at the snowmen smiling, smiling, La de, etc.

    Jolly and fat, oh! scarves and hat, La de, etc.

3   Look at the robins hopping, hopping, La de, etc.

    Robin redbreast, oh! fly from your nest, La de, etc.

4   Look at the skaters gliding, gliding, La de, etc.

    Slides and whirls, oh! jumps and twirls, La de, etc.

Something to think about

Can you think of someone who won't get many cards this Christmas? Make a special card and send it to them.

Suggestion

Look at some Christmas cards and add more verses.

Accompaniment

Pitched percussion or recorders

Christmas customs

61   Ring, bells, ring!
62   Christmas bells
63   I am Father Christmas
64   When Santa got stuck up the chimney
65   Jingle bells

61
Ring, bells, ring!

Narrative

Bells are also common on Christmas cards. They ring out on Christmas morning. People in the Holy Land like to hear the bells from the Church of the Nativity. This church is built on the spot where the stable stood in Bethlehem.

Words and music by
David Moses

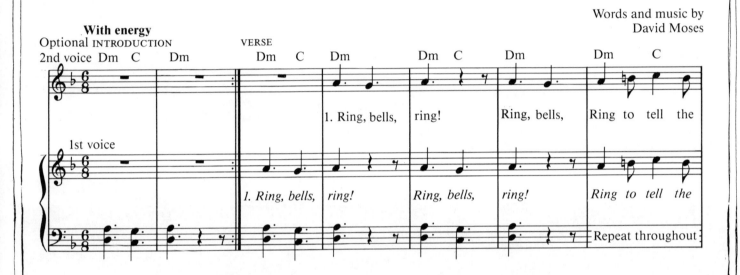

morn - ing that a child was born in Beth - le - hem. Three Wise

Men fol - lowed the star and came to see the child in Beth - le -

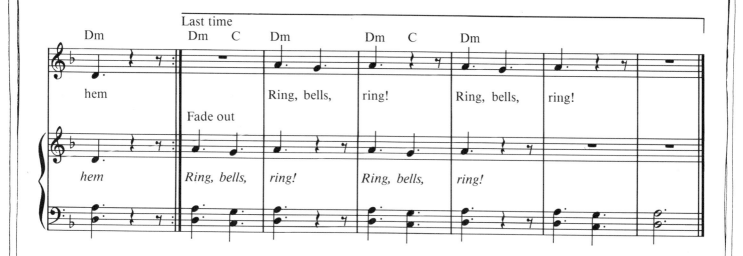

2 Ring, bells, ring! Ring, bells, ring!

Ring to tell the morning that a child was born in a manger cold.

Angels told shepherds to come and play the pipe and drum for the baby boy.

Ring, bells, ring! Ring, bells, ring!

Activity

Make a piece out of different sorts of bell sounds –
Indian cymbals, chime bars, triangles and so on.

Accompaniment

Pitched percussion and recorders choose from
these patterns:

Repeat throughout.

62
Christmas bells

Narrative

The bells ring out a time of peace. Christmas is an important time in people's search for peace. The angels sang: 'Peace on earth, goodwill to everyone'.

At Christmas time people dream of a world with no more war. Several times in history Christmas has been a time when a war has ceased, either for a short period or for good.

One Christmas during the Second World War,

enemies became friends for a while. Two American soldiers knocked at the door of a German house asking for help for a French soldier. All three were invited in, and were followed by German soldiers who were also invited in. Together they ate a meal. The next day the Germans helped the American and French soldiers find their way back to their army.

Words and music by
Zoe McHenry

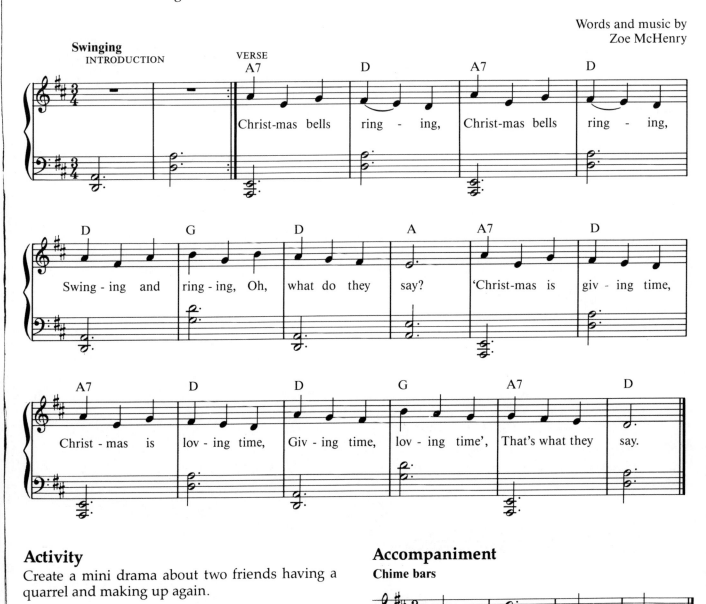

Activity

Create a mini drama about two friends having a quarrel and making up again.

Accompaniment

Chime bars

Repeat throughout starting with the voices

116

63
I am Father Christmas

Narrative

In many European countries St Nicholas is an important part of Christmas. He was a friendly German saint who died on the 6th of December about 1600 years ago. The legend tells that he was fond of children. In his country some people were so poor that sometimes mothers and fathers had to sell the children to be slaves. St Nicholas heard about one family who had to sell their three daughters so that the rest of the family would be able to live. So each night for three nights St Nicholas crept up to their window and threw in a bag of gold to save the daughters, one by one.

In some countries St Nicholas (or Santa Claus, as we call him) comes on the 6th of December, three weeks before Christmas. In Holland, he arrives on a ship from Spain with a horse and his friend Black Peter. He wears a long red cloak and a bishop's hat. Black Peter wears velvet trousers and a hat with a feather. He walks on the rooftops, searching out children who have been good. He drops sweets and gifts down chimneys into the children's shoes which they put out for him to fill. Black Peter carries the gifts, but he also has a sack to carry away children who have been really bad.

Words and music by
Monica Shelton

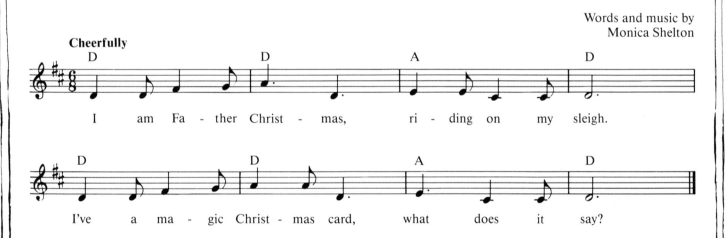

I am Fa - ther Christ - mas, ri - ding on my sleigh.

I've a ma - gic Christ - mas card, what does it say?

Suggestion

Play this as a question and answer game. The answering child sings or says a made-up answer.

64
When Santa got stuck up the chimney

Narrative

Many countries have someone who brings gifts secretly. In France, 'Père Noel' arrives on a donkey putting gifts in shoes. In China he is called 'Lan Khoong-Khoong', which means 'nice old father'. In Japan he is called 'Hoteiosho' and he has eyes in the back of his head to watch how children behave. Arab children look forward to the 'Littlest Camel' bringing gifts. In Costa Rica 'el Niño' – the Christ child himself – brings gifts. In Chile he is called 'Viejo Pascuero' and arrives with reindeer.

In Brazil several people may come. In some homes Papa Noel (Father Christmas) arrives by helicopter. In other parts Santa Claus arrives dressed in red suit and boots with artificial snow, even though it is the hottest part of the year in Brazil. In other places the three Kings bring presents.

In this song Santa has trouble with his delivery of presents.

Words and music by
Jimmy Grafton

65
Jingle bells

Narrative

When the Dutch people travelled to America they took their customs with them. In America St Nicholas is called Santa Claus. He rides in a sledge in the sky with reindeer, and lives at the North Pole. The children in America used to wear laced leather shoes. These could not be filled up with presents very easily, so the children left out stockings instead.

Capo 1st fret

Happily

Traditional

Alternative version

VERSE
Christmas time is near

And we are off to bed.
As we climb the stairs

We nod our sleepy heads.

We take our stockings off,

And hang them in a row,
And then jump quickly into bed
And off to sleep we go.

CHORUS
Jingle bells, jingle bells,
Jingle all the way!

Santa Claus is coming soon,
Riding in his sleigh.
Jingle bells, jingle bells,
Jingle all the way!

Hurrah for dear old Santa Claus!

Hurrah for Christmas Day.

Activity

Make up a piece based on bells, using jingle bells as an ostinato.

120

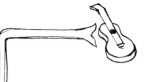

Parties
and food

66   Christmas Eve in Trinidad
67   It's Christmas Day
68   Welcome here!
69   We wish you a Merry Christmas

66
Christmas Eve in Trinidad

Narrative

In Trinidad on Christmas Eve the Parang singers sing songs accompanied by guitars, banjos and homemade musical instruments. Sometimes they go from house to house and sometimes they stay in one place. People give them cakes and sweet breads in return for their singing.

On Christmas Eve too, people do their baking. They make cakes and boil hams. A favourite dish is *pastelles*. These are rather like English pasties and consist of meat inside a pastry made of cornflour.

Their favourite drink is sorrel. This is made from the petals of a small red flower, which is pulled apart and covered with boiling water. Then sugar and cinnamon are added.

In Trinidad, Christmas is a time for visiting families and friends. Father Christmas comes and leaves presents under the Christmas tree.

Listen to the song. What don't they have in Port of Spain? (Port of Spain is the main city of Trinidad.)

Words and music by
Massie Patterson and
Sammy Heyward

Calypso style

VERSE

San - ta what you do-in' Christ-mas Eve? At me house what are you goin' to leave?_

San - ta how you goin' to make the rein-deer go? In Port of Spain San-ta we don't have snow.

CHORUS

Christ-mas Eve in Tri - ni - dad,_ Child-ren are good not one is bad.._

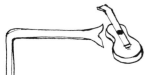

What a night for girls and boys! Santa will bring them plenty of toys.

Suggestion

Make up other verses about Christmas in other parts of the world.

Accompaniment

Add unpitched percussion in a calypso rhythm.

Repeat throughout.

Add pitched percussion or recorders to the chorus:

Pitched percussion and recorders for chorus

67
It's Christmas Day

Narrative

Christmas parties are the chance for families and friends to get together to enjoy themselves. Old quarrels are forgotten (sometimes!) and we make a special effort to be with people we do not often see.

We often pull crackers at Christmas parties. Crackers were invented in 1850 by a London sweet-maker called Tom Smith, who sold sweets and small toys wrapped in fancy paper. As he watched the sparks and cracks coming from his log fire, he thought how good it would be if his packages made a crack when the wrapping was pulled apart. It took him two years to design his first cracker.

People used to play special games at Christmas parties. Some were quite dangerous, like 'Snap-dragon'. A pewter dish was filled with spirit and set alight. Currants were scattered on it. The game was to snatch the currants out of the flames and put them in your mouth. 'Blind man's buff', where a blindfolded person tried to catch someone, was also popular. In 'Hunt the slipper' a shoe was hidden and people had to look for it.

The game of 'Forfeits' was like 'Pass the parcel'. In between each layer of paper there was a small piece of paper on which the forfeit was written. The person who unwrapped it would have to do something funny, like standing on his/her head.

Twelfth Night (6th January) was a time for parties too. At these the 'Lord of Misrule' was chosen to lead the merry-making. Pieces of Twelfth Night cake were cut. The person who got the piece containing a dried pea or bean was 'Lord of Misrule'. He had a fancy costume and everybody had to obey him. He carried a bladder blown up on the end of a stick and hit people with it. This is probably how balloons came to be invented.

Huddie Ledbetter,
adapted by
June Tillman

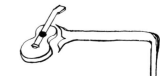

5 My balloon's just popped, etc.

6 Munch a piece of cake, etc.

7 Now we're playing games, etc.

8 Let's play 'Pass the parcel', etc.

9 Let's play 'Blind man's buff', etc.

Suggestion

Adapt this carol as you wish.

Alternative version

1 Chickens crowing from midnight, it's almost day, etc.

2 Santa Claus is coming, it's almost day, etc.

3 Hang your stockings up, etc.

4 Candy bars and sugar sweets, etc.

5 We're peeping round the corner, etc.

6 Chickens crowing from midnight, etc.

Accompaniment

Pitched percussion

125

68
Welcome here!

Narrative

All over the world and throughout history certain foods have been been popular at Christmas time. In Finland, families cook gingerbread in the shape of stars, figures, animals and homes. In Greece, children are given nuts and fruits at the end of the service on Christmas Eve. At Christmas parties in Holland chestnuts are eaten. They are boiled and eaten with salt and butter. In old England the pig's head was the centre of the Christmas feast. People also enjoyed geese, beef, mutton, pork, pheasant, swan, rabbit, oysters, and a peacock splendidly decorated with its own feathers.

There was beer, and pear and apple cider to drink. Some beer was flavoured with spices from the East. In the seventeenth century, at the time of Oliver Cromwell, the Puritans tried to stop all feasting and for some years Christmas was not celebrated. But it was too popular to disappear for long.

A century later, turkeys became common in Britain after people had been to America, because the turkey was an American bird. Pulling the turkey or chicken wishbone is a very old custom. Two people each hold one end of the wishbone and pull. As the bone breaks the person with the longer piece makes a wish. This will only come true if no one talks or laughs while the bone is being pulled. And the wish must be kept secret!

Mince pies were originally mutton pies and were oval in shape like Jesus' cradle. In some places it is considered unlucky to refuse one. Some people make a wish when they take the first bite. (See also Dame get up and bake your pies, page 16.)

Traditional American

With gusto

CHORUS

Wel - come here, wel - come here, All be a - live and of good cheer. of good cheer.

VERSE

1. I've got a pie all baked com - plete, Pud - ding too that's ve - ry sweet.

D.C. al fine

Chest - nuts are roast - ing; join us here, While we dance and make good cheer.

2 I've got a log that's burning hot,
Toddy's bubbling in the pot.
Come in ye people where it's warm,
Winds blow sharp and it may storm.

CHORUS Welcome here, etc.

3 I made a loaf that's cooling there,
With my neighbours I will share.
Come all ye people, hear me sing,
Songs of friendly welcoming.

CHORUS Welcome here, etc.

Additional verses

4   I've made some mince pies, piping hot;
     Pudding's boiling in the pot.

     Soon it will be carried in

     Smelling good and flaming.

     CHORUS   Welcome here, etc.

5   I've got a turkey fat and good,
     Stuffed with chestnuts from the wood.

     Roast potatoes all around,
     Hear the sizzling baking sound.

     CHORUS   Welcome here, etc.

6   Roasting in the stove is swan,
     Peacock fills the dish it's on,

     Scent of spices fills the air;
     Have a great big glass of beer.

     CHORUS   Welcome here, etc.

Suggestion

The last three verses have been added to the traditional ones. Make up some more about other foods.

Accompaniment

This is a pentatonic tune based on the scale:

Make up accompaniments using these notes,

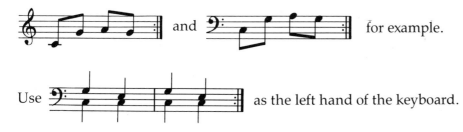 for example.

Use   as the left hand of the keyboard.

69

We wish you a Merry Christmas

Narrative

The Christmas pudding was originally a soup made from beef, mutton, raisins, currants, prunes and wine. Today we use currants, raisins and sultanas instead of prunes, but suet, breadcrumbs, eggs and spices are still there. We often stick a piece of holly in the pudding and pour brandy or rum over it and set it alight. The pudding is often the climax of the Christmas meal.

Meals are important at Christmas time and at other festivals all over the world. They are a time of getting together for families and friends, when old quarrels are forgotten. They are a time of happiness and peace, when we wish people well for the coming year. They are the end of all our preparations.

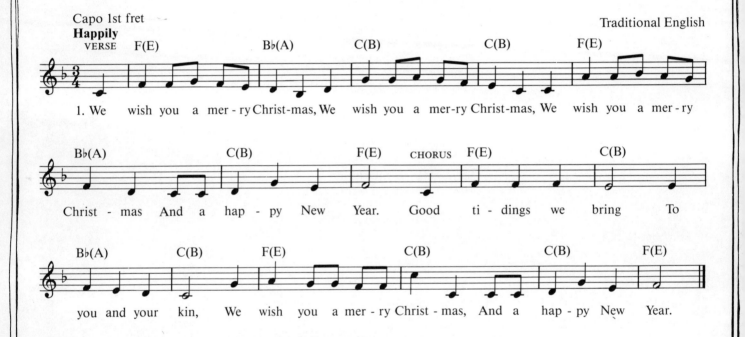

2 Now bring us some figgy pudding (three times)
   And bring some out here.

   CHORUS   Good tidings we bring, etc.

3 We all like our figgy pudding (three times)
   With all its good cheer.

   CHORUS   Good tidings we bring, etc.

4 We won't go until we've got some (three times)
   So bring some out here.

   CHORUS   Good tidings we bring, etc.

Accompaniment

Add a tambourine playing ‖: ♩ ♩ :‖ throughout.